SOLDIER 4346057

"SHORT, THEREFORE, IS MAN'S LIFE AND NARROW THE CORNER OF THE EARTH WHEREIN HE DWELLS." *Anon.*

It is my hope that this narrative, with scrapbook, will be preserved by our children if for no other reason than to ensure they do not forget the tragedy which fell not only on England and Europe but on the whole world, and that they do not forget also the absolute futility of war.

DEDICATION

To my dear late wife, Margaret, daughters, Susan and Jane,
grandchildren, Katie, Adam, Paul and Robert,
and all those who never returned.

THE SECOND WORLD WAR

11 a.m., 3 September 1939 to 2.41 a.m., 8 May 1945 (Europe)

4346057 – Hudson, D.

Age on entry – twenty-one years (army)

The notes contained in this book are a verbatim copy of those taken by me during military service. They were in pencil, on paper once white but now sepia-coloured with the passing years; before my memory fades, like the notes, concerning certain details and dates, the transcribing to type was commenced as a New Year's resolution.

Where possible the notes are supported by a scrapbook of pictures and press cuttings, most of which I was able to secrete home for safekeeping in the monthly allowance of one green envelope (applicable to duty overseas). Green envelopes were subject only to spot checks by censors as opposed to unit mail, all of which was censored before leaving the unit. Green envelopes were censored at base by persons unknown to the writer.

The notes comprise a potpourri of anecdotes, hopes and fears, successes and failures of the Herculean days of war. As I read them now, more than five decades later, they do seem a little melodramatic or histrionic, but I am sure that at the time any attempt to create such an impression could not have been further from my mind. The attendant difficulties and danger in compiling these notes, often hidden away in my kit in a rear echelon, does bring back a little nostalgia. Whilst not representing top-grade intelligence, if a rear HQ had been overrun and the notes captured, they would without doubt have been of some use to the enemy.

I wrote as I felt, as I thought and as I saw, believing strongly that right was on our side and that the Almighty would give us all the priceless experience of witnessing a victory at some time and that we would, as Rupert Brooke wrote in the First World War, 'see the powers of darkness put to flight'. We did indeed see the morning break and the glorious light of freedom which followed, always remembering those less fortunate ones who were not so privileged.

RANK, COURSES AND PROMOTIONS

Private Soldier	15 January 1940
Acting Unpaid Lance Corporal	2 July 1940
Lance Corporal	31 October 1940
Full Corporal	3 December 1940
Lance Sergeant	4 November 1941
Sergeant	1 January 1942
War Substantive Sergeant (Signals)	1 April 1942

Basic Infantry Training	Beverley, East Yorks.
Advanced Field Training	Beverley, West Woods
Specialist Signals (Infantry)	Hornsea, East Yorks.
Wireless/Telegraphy	Seaburn, Co. Durham
Signals, Classified Q1	Catterick, North Yorks.
10 Corps Junior Leaders School: Pass Q1	Leyburn, North Yorks.
Bofors 40-mm AA Gunnery: Pass Q1	Chester, Cheshire
Aircraft Recognition: Pass Q1	Hoo, nr Chatham, Kent
Mines: Pass Q1	Hoo
Motor Transport: Pass Q2	Hoo
Junior Commando: Pass Q1	San Martino, Italy
Signals Refresher: Pass Q1	Paolisi, Italy

MOVEMENTS, UNITS AND FORMATIONS

I volunteered for the Royal Air Force on Sunday 3 September 1939 at a recruiting office in the Odeon Cinema, The Mount. Scores were being turned away on arrival and told to wait for registration. I joined the long queue nevertheless and an officer came to talk to us on the pavement. He explained that there were few training establishments, no equipment and few instructors; and that if we volunteered for flying duties, it would make no difference. Eventually I made it to a trestle table in the foyer and was again told exactly what the officer had said, so I went home to wait.

Royal proclamation, age group 20/22	1 October 1939
Registered. Order of choice: RAF, navy, army	21 October 1939
Medical examination, St George's Cinema, Castlegate, York	11 November 1939
Papers received for the army	6 January 1940
East Yorks. Regt., Training Depot, Beverley Barracks	15 January 1940
Signals Depot, Hornsea, East Yorks.	14 April 1940
Conservative Club, Beverley	29 June 1940
8th Bn. East Yorks. Regt., XV Foot, HQ Coy, Sunderland	11 October 1940
D Coy, Horden, Co. Durham	31 October 1940
HQ Coy, Seaburn, nr Sunderland	10 December 1940
B Coy, No. 11 Platoon, Roker Park, Sunderland	27 December 1940
Seaburn	11 January 1941
HQ Coy (Signals), Sunderland	11 February 1941
Wireless/telegraphy course, Seaburn	16 February 1941
10 Corps Junior Leaders School, Leyburn, North Yorks.	16 March 1941
Sunderland	26 April 1941

Hutton Rudby, North Yorks.	12 May 1941
West Hartlepool, Co. Durham	1 August 1941
Middlesbrough	23 November 1941
Chester	29 December 1941
Carnforth, Lancs.	24 February 1942
Dover, Kent	24 March 1942
Hoo, nr Chatham, Kent	7 April 1942
Ashford, Kent	25 April 1942
Hawkinge, Folkestone, Kent	10 May 1942
Butlin's Camp, Clacton, Essex	18 July 1942
Shorncliffe, Kent	28 July 1942
Stubbington, Hants	30 July 1942
Folkestone, Kent	12 August 1942
Ashford	21 August 1942
Clacton, Essex	23 September 1942
Ashford	6 October 1942
Aldershot, Hants	4 December 1942
Embarkation leave	15–18 December 1942
King George V Dock, Liverpool	23 December 1942
Mersey estuary	24 December 1942
Set sail for Clyde	25 December 1942
Algiers, North Africa	3 January 1943
Sidi Moussa	4 January 1943
Souhk Arras	12 January 1943
Ghardimaou	13 January 1943
Tabarka, Tunisia	20 January 1943
Sedjenane (West)	24 January 1943
Battle of the Ridge, Sedjenane	30 January 1943
Battle for Sedjenane	28 February 1943
Djebel Abiod	5 March 1943
Three days' rest, Tabarka	20 March 1943
Concentration area, nr Djebel Abiod	24 March 1943
Djebel Abiod recaptured	25 March 1943
Nr Sedjenane	4 April 1943

139th Brigade, 46th British Division, 1st Army was at this stage considerably depleted and we were merged with the remnants of some commando units and the Parachute Brigade, operating under the title of the latter in 46th Division until 139th Brigade was reformed.

Our route took us through Tabarka, Ain Draham, Fermana, Souhk-el-Chemis, Souhk-el-Aba, le Krib and El Aroussa to Central Sector Northern Front to provide support in the Kasserine Gap battle.

Kasserine Gap battle	14 April 1943
Medjes-el-Bab	20 April 1943
Hideout (place not recorded)	22 April 1943
Goubelat Plain – final attack on Tunis	22 April 1943
Hideout in a wadi with 138th Brigade	23 April 1943
Bouarada	30 April 1943
Across Goubelat Plain and fall of Tunis	7 May 1943
Hideout, Medjes-Oued-Zarga	10 May 1943
Hamman Lif	4 June 1943
Beaufarik, nr Algiers	16 June 1943
Blida	17 July 1943
Hussen Day	9 August 1943
Embarked, HMT *Ban Fora*, Algiers	11 August 1943
Fast sail, in 3-mile limit with one escort, Bizerte	13 August 1943
Embarked, LST (landing ship for tanks) 371	7 September 1943
Salerno Landing, Green Beach, zero plus 16 hours	9 September 1943
Ten days elapsed before beach secure	not recorded
Ponte Cignano	24 September 1943
Nocera	4 October 1943
Pompeii, nr Naples	6 October 1943
Plain of Naples, Villa Literno	8 October 1943
Crossing of River Volturno	14 October 1943
Francolise	26 October 1943
Four days' rest, Salerno	22 November 1943
Auto Strada 7, Concha, nr Rochamonfina	12 December 1943
Vezzaro, nr Cassino	17 December 1943
Valley below River Garigliano, Cassino	8 January 1944

At this point 46th British Division had had 110 per cent replacement of officers and terrible punishment in casualties. We had been in action or in a front area with only four days' rest in the shambles of Salerno since the landing on 9 September. Tired, exceedingly jumpy and virtually a spent force, it was just too much, living in or out of the line under the shadow of the monster Cassino. We handed over all our remaining equipment to Polish and Canadian units, who finally tackled Monte Cassino.

Proceeded to Naples	21 February 1944
Embarked, HMT *Sobieski* (captured Polish transport)	21 February 1944
Port Said, Egypt	27 February 1944
Quassassin, nr Tel-el-Kebir	28 February 1944
Leave, Cairo	12 March 1944
Nathanya, Palestine	18 March 1944
Tel Aviv	24 March 1944
Hadera	8 April 1944
Haifa	15 April 1944
Exercises (Greek Navy mutiny; security), Nahariya	7 May 1944
Hadera	14 May 1944
Jerusalem	18 May 1944
Bethlehem and Nablus	19 May 1944
Camp Tahag, Quassassin	16 June 1944
Transit camp, Amiyra	24 June 1944
Alexandria	26 June 1944
Sailed from Alexandria, HMT *Derbyshire*	29 June 1944
Taranto, Southern Italy	3 July 1944
Fitting out, Nassissi	5 July 1944
Concentration area, Caserta	6 July 1944
Bavagna	20 July 1944
Staging area, Rome	21 July 1944
Via Foligno, Belmonte, Casanova, Serravalle and Macerata to the East Coast Sector of 18th Army Group, British 8th Army	15 August 1944
Fabriano and Sessa Ferrato	23 August 1944
San Lorenzo – Gothic Line	24 August 1944
Sapriano	29 August 1944
Golendino	3 September 1944

Salleducia and Il Peggio	5 September 1944
Montefiore	10 September 1944
Vallechio	19 September 1944
Serravello	21 September 1944
Dognana	6 October 1944
La Villa – River Marrechia	6 October 1944
Santarcangelo	9 October 1944
Mondiano (heaviest losses)	14 October 1944
Three days' rest, Taveleto	18 October 1944
Fano, Senigallia	21 October 1944
Bertinoro	31 October 1944
San Vittore and Fratta	5 November 1944
Falerone in Forenzia	9 November 1944
Via Foligno, Terni, Rome, Cassino and Capua to Naples	1 December 1944
6th Battalion IRTD (infantry reinforcement training), Paolisi	5 December 1944
4th Battalion IRTD (advanced field training), San Martino	4 February 1945
Junior Commando Course (six weeks)	—
Signals IRTD, Depot HQ	18 March 1945
Seven days' leave, Bari	29 March 1945
Staff IRTD instructor, Depot HQ	10 April 1945
Italian War ceasefire	3 May 1945
Seven days' leave, Isle of Ischia	2 June 1945
Rome, Ancona, Venice and Mestre	15 July 1945
CRU (Corps Reinforcement Unit), No. 2 British, Udine	16 July 1945
10th Indian Division, 4th Foot, 1st Bn King's Own Royal Regt.	—
Internal security, attached 14/16th Garwhali Rifles, Gorizia	7 August 1945
Seven days' leave, The Lido, Venice	29 August 1945
Land LIAP (leave in addition to *Python*), England	15 September 1945
Arrived at Folkestone	19 September 1945
Calais to Bolzano via Switzerland, Milan and Verona	26 October 1945
24th Guards Brigade, 56th Division, Lazeretto, nr Trieste	29 December 1945
Yugoslav Border Guards, Trieste and Muggia	5 February 1946
Class 'A' Release Group 26	28 March 1946

Journey Home

Transport from Trieste to Udine; train to Milan, Villach, Seebach, Malnitz, Salzburg, Traunstein, Rosenheim, Munich, Augsburg, Ulm, Karmenstein, Karlsruhe, Strasbourg, Pagnym, Hirson, Lille, Armentières and Calais; train from Dover to Aldershot, Woking, King's Cross and York.

PART ONE: ENGLAND

15 January 1940 to 24 December 1942

15th January 1940: Mother woke me far too early so as not to 'miss the train' or get 'into trouble'. Typical, but I didn't say anything. I was only going to Beverley and had about four hours to get the train, living only a mile from the station. Had a huge breakfast of porridge, bacon and egg, tomato and fried bread and gallons of tea and toast. Mother tried to hold back the tears and I did not look at her but I had to do on leaving the house. She cried a little and gave me a small New Testament to fit my back pocket. Father and Blagdon saw me off and Enid looked in at the station but could not wait for the train. Met Bert Darley as arranged. No-one to see him off. Lovely sky, a breeze and thick white clouds darting about.

In Beverley Station a blackboard was propped up against a trolley and on it were the words "Recruits East Yorks – Wait here". The first command, I thought. A Sergeant appeared. I did not like him. Lined up in threes and he swore at us a few times. We were all over the place. He did not exactly endear himself to us when he said "Bloody hell, this lot can't count. Threes I said". He has a lot of ribbons on his chest and looks like the devil incarnate. Perhaps he is. He would not even let us talk as we entered the barrack gates. We are a weird looking lot with cases, carrier bags and parcels.

17th January 1940: long queue in six inches of snow for kit. Never worn long pants but had to take one of everything on a list given to us by a Quartermaster. Boots weigh half a ton and

14

I shall be ashamed to go out in my battle-dress, if we ever get out of this place from what we hear. Far too big but there was nothing else. The denims are better but you can't go out of the barracks in them. There are no rifles or steel helmets.

18th January 1940: issued with Army Pass Book. I am 4346057. 434 stands for the Regiment of East Yorkshires. Sgt says this number will be engraved on our hearts until we die which will be sooner than we think if we do not pay attention to him all the time. Charming fellow this one. Twice as ignorant as the one who met us at the station. He says our Mothers will not know us in a few weeks. He says he is our Mother and Brother from now on. He then took us to the large hall to be sworn in and have some of the King's Regulations read out to us.

19th January 1940: always blowing the bugle for some reason. Suppose we shall be told in due time what they all mean. God help us with this Sgt if we get them mixed up. I know 'reveille'. It starts on a note fit to give you a heart attack and goes on like eternity. This morning another Sgt, not seen before, with a red sash across his front dashed in to the barrack room almost before the last echo had died away, shouting "Rise and shine, beds in line, arse 'oles to the front". A very uncouth way to start the day. Anyone who did not move he pushed out. Early breakfast this week – 0630 a.m. More snow.

22nd January 1940: end of week one. Feet hurt with boots. No-one allowed out yet which is just as well as I couldn't walk to Beverley. Only three of us in our room wear pyjamas so we are called cissies. Everyone seems to sleep in their shirt they wear during the day. Decided to post pyjamas home at first opportunity and sleep in shirt from now on.

24th January 1940: lectures on army formations and general information. Because we are on late breakfast this week we have to do P.T. whilst first meal is on. Mug of hot cocoa first. There are so many of us in this unit we have to take it in turns to go to the gym and this morning was our turn to be outside in the snow – in the dark in what must have been zero temperatures. I managed to get half under the shed. Crazy.

2nd February 1940: had to parade at Guard House for inspection before being allowed out for the first time. Geoff Rawlings and I were turned back because we had scarves under our great-coats. Big fat pug-nosed Sgt we had never seen before said we were 'improperly dressed'. It was a long way back to the barrack so we made the fatal mistake and argued. I said my battle-dress was so big round the neck there was a draught. I was promptly told to shut up and get out. I did. We appeared again later and pug-nose let us out but too late to go to the pictures. Had half a pint. Long trudge back in the snow. Lovely clear night.

8th February 1940: did bayonet training today. Had to run at a sack of sawdust suspended on a bar. We had to shout and scream like wild animals, stab the thing twice and dash back, not dawdle, to the starting place. Hands inspected afterwards for blood. If any showed between the thumb and first finger it meant the rifle was not held properly. We were all bleeding. Sgt went quite mad. He ran like a wild thing at the sack, stabbed it half a dozen times and flew back like the wind proudly showing us there was no blood on his hands. Charlie Beer a rough diamond from Hull if ever there was one said Sgt was used to it and we were not. A most unfortunate remark and he was nearly done for insubordination.

[*Undated*:] Issued with our own rifles for keeps. Mine is a short butt Lee Enfield stamped 1918. Number J.33158. Sgt says, next to himself, this is our best friend.

11th February 1940: passed first TOETs (Test of Elementary Training).

14th February 1940: had first shots with rifle. Missed target completely twice but otherwise not bad. Had some inners but no bulls.

The author on his final leave, December 1942.

Retreat, Venice, March 1945.

Trieste Bay, scuttled ships, March 1944.

Yugoslav border, March 1944.

Rhine, March 1946.

The author in the grounds of the Conservative Club, August 1940.

Near Salerno, Italy.

Mount of Olives, overlooking the Garden of Gethsemane, May 1944.

Church of All Nations, May 1944.

Austria, March 1946.

21

Italian border, March 1944.

Alexandria. April 1944.

Jeneseit, near Bolzano, 1945.

The Lido, Venice, August 1945. The author is on the left.

American club, The Lido, Venice.

Mount George Island, Venice.

Switzerland, March 1946.

15th February 1940: trouble on pay parade. This was the first one in the large drill hall. There is another 57 in another company and also by the same surname. We both stepped forward when the QM shouted "Hudson 57". The last digits only are called. Who the other chap was I do not know. The whole parade was stunned to silence as the RSM shouted "get back". We did so promptly. The same shout came from the QM. "Hudson 57" and again we both stepped forward. Now the RSM was angry. He shouted, louder still and louder asking if one of us was deaf. We stood there rigidly to attention. This is the end I thought. We shall both be shot. Dead silence. Situation saved by a young Lieut. who came down the line and told us both to fall out and fall in again at the end of the alphabet with the Ys. I then found out that George Hudson was 4345957 from Hull and in another company and I am 6057. Because we had to wait until the end, the last two or three letters of the alphabet were caught for coal fatigues for the officers' mess and this went on until well into the evening so it was too late to go out. Finished my pocket money from home so feel quite rich. Two bob a day retrospective to 15th January, less credits.

16th February 1940: lessons on Bren gun and 2" mortar.

17th February 1940: had some inoculations and allowed 48 hours excused duty. T.A.B. Big lump coming underneath the armpit and arm stiff. Don't feel very well. Syd Micklefield who sleeps next to me is really ill but nobody seems to bother. His forehead is steaming like an early morning fog. Sgt says you often develop a vaccine fever, not to worry as it wears off.

20th February 1940: although effect of inoculations not worn off yet we had to go on a route march. Sgt made us swing both arms – which we could not do – and anyone who made a feeble attempt had a great clout by the wrists from a huge twig he pulled from a hedge. I suppose he thought this was funny. He went up and down the column like a mad thing so when he passed you, the arms hung limp but he would suddenly turn round as if he knew the trick and come back and – clout. Wilf Frain wanted to lodge an official complaint but we felt we were all too new at the game to say or do much.

23rd February 1940: more practice firing. Lay on the range next to Casey who put all his application shots on my target and none on his own. I had 20 shots on mine instead of 10. He got 7 days on the spot which apparently can be done for this offence under King's Regulations. We had to stay behind to fire application again. All the butts being free I got up and moved along, well away from Casey and Sgt played pop. He made us fire on adjacent targets yet all the rest were empty.

4th March 1940: field craft. Had to take turns in being in charge of a section to move up a hill unnoticed and capture an objective on the top. We were told an NCO would be at the top watching to detect any noise or movement. We had to report to an officer as if we had been to a proper 'O' group and give the object, the intention, the method, communications etc. When it was my turn to go, we moved off along the half mile straight before moving up the hill and I saw an empty coal cart coming along, so we stopped him and asked for a lift right round to the other side of the hill. We lay covered in coal dust and he was only too pleased to help. We were then able to creep up the hill behind the object and take him by surprise. We were told not to fix bayonets but we made the wild screams as taught when at the top. Who should be sitting there on a log but old pug face from the guard room incident. He was livid. Asked who was in charge, took my name and number. When we went to a lecture on all the faults etc., I got no marks and a rollicking on the grounds that in war time there would be no coal cart and that most probably the reverse side of the hill would be enemy territory. So after all a bit of initiative is not always the right thing. Sgt says we are in the Army to do as we are told which meant to approach the hill as directed and not to think of alternatives.

11th March 1940: our platoon mounted guard tonight to drum and bugle. Not one word of command spoken. The rest of the barracks watched and we were complimented by the C.O. Bitterly cold. Allowed balaclavas on duty. On middle turn, main gate. Made all the top brass show their passes/identity.

18th March 1940: more shooting on range. Did better than before but missed some snap shooting. Had to run 100 yards and then down for five snap shots but the target only stayed up for 5 seconds. I only hit two out of my five and had to shoot again. Sgt said on the way back that none of us will live very long unless we improve on the range. He said we were in the Army not only to learn how to kill Germans but also how to survive and not be killed ourselves and one way of doing this was to be quicker than the other chap. He is better for knowing is the Sgt. Salt of the earth I suppose in the peace time army. He got most of his medals on the Indian Frontier.

23rd March 1940: two out of our platoon selected for interview as possible candidates for an RASC OCTU. Self and Bert Darley. I could not answer any of the questions about the internal combustion engine although I said I knew how to drive. I had to admit I could not strip an engine. Bert's father runs a garage in York and he gave the right answers so was chosen to go forward to the next stage. Sgt played pop outside for saying I did not know anything about engines. Fat lot of good that would have been if I had been asked to strip an engine when I got there. Bert thinks he will go to Bournemouth.

26th March 1940: sent for to Orderly Room this morning. Told I was going with Geoff Rawlings to Hornsea on a specialist Infantry Signalman's course for three months coupled with some field training.

29th March 1940: Enid, my sister, came to see me today. Lovely and sunny. Walked in the Westwoods and racecourse and had a picnic. Some of Mother's specials.

10th April 1940: allowed out for full day and hitch hiked home all in one lift for a few hours. Had to have three lifts back and only just made it in time.

[*Undated*:] Morse, morse and more morse practice. Also learning to operate heliograph when the sun shines. Field cable laying exercises and lectures on the field telephone and fullerphone. This is the gadget where you cannot tap in to intercept a message.

15th May 1940: tests on flag signalling, morse and field telephone.

[*Undated*:] all last few weeks on tests, morse, lectures and cable laying. We are getting some speeds now.

28th June 1940: classified as an Infantry Signaller and given our crossed flags to wear on the left lower forearm.

29th June 1940: whole course moved to Beverley. Had to walk from Hornsea in FSMO (Field Service Marching Order). Longest route march yet. When on the outskirts of Beverley some unit attacked us. It was a Company attack from the left – no warning – and our C.O. who was walking with us said he knew nothing about it the lying hound. We were just about all in after walking from Hornsea. We had to go to a lecture afterwards and were all criticised for not reacting quickly enough to the element of surprise. We would all have been either killed or taken prisoner according to the C.O. This unit had flash bombs, fired blank flares etc. and were obviously enjoying putting into practice some of their own training. We found out later they were a unit of the York and Lancs and we noted this for future reference.

30th June 1940: foot inspection by M.O. No blisters. Billet in Conservative Club. Rest all day.

[*Undated*:] First news of air raids on London by day. Anti-invasion lectures and frequent exercises by day and night. If an invasion takes place the bells of the Minster and all Churches will ring. We have rehearsed so many times, we know where to go blind folded but all we seem to have are Brens and rifles and one Bren carrier.

4th August 1940: some Lewis machine guns arrived and another carrier.

10th August 1940: air battles mounting over London are being called "The Battle of Britain". Some activity at night over Hull. Our old barracks outside Beverley bombed. Armoury hit and some killed. Wonder where old pug face was. Our training Sgt is O.K.

21st August 1940: all leave cancelled. Not had mine yet. More night exercises.

[*Undated, September 1940*:] Air raids increasing over London. Many casualties. Day after day, exercises, new situations, lectures, route marches, P.T. and revision of field, tactical and signal training. Heavy losses both sides over Kent.

15th October 1940: moved few days ago to Seaburn, Nr. Sunderland, Co. Durham. New Bn formed, the 8Bn East Yorks. Smashing billet in a private house with George Foster and Ernie Towse. All the platoon of 30 men in one house. No straw yet for palliasses so sleep on bare boards. Sea front always deserted but found a small cafe open at night for two hours and they put some records on for George and I. He is mad on dance music.

17th October 1940: put on beach defences all day. Rumour has it, all next week as well. Issued with thick gloves for unrolling barbed wire and stakes. All mined in front of wire so we had to pay attention and move with wire in groups at a time. Bitterly cold.

21st October 1940: first night allowed out for long time. Went to pictures in Fawcett St., Sunderland with George. Got caught outside by Military Police for being improperly dressed. Our unit has to wear caps dead centre of the head and we had them on at the usual slant and also our top buttons undone. I told the Cpl it was hot in the pictures and he told me to shut up. George said it was chilly first thing down on the beach and was nearly done for impertinence. Our names, numbers and unit were taken. No other unit wears their caps like we do. Fad of the C.O.

31st October 1940: a great day in the life of Private Hudson. I became an acting unpaid lance corporal this morning. The lowest of the low. My pay goes up 1/6d a day when I get paid. Wonder when that will be. The CSM lost no time in giving me my first job and I did not like it one bit. I have always been drilled and it was odd having to drill others and I was told to take some men as a relief squad to the beaches complete with weapons, tools to follow, to dig some observation post above the beach. Someone down there would tell me where.

We set off in the height of the afternoon leaving traffic down Fawcett St., the main road in Sunderland. Everyone seemed very understanding as I halted the squad sometimes too early and sometimes too late at traffic lights. Nearly at the end of Fawcett St., I saw some top brass on the pavement just standing watching. Could not see their rank but they had red tabs on so when we were about opposite, we marched to attention and I saluted followed by a smart "eyes left" and then at ease. Then I heard footsteps running behind me – I was at the rear of the squad – and what appeared to be a Staff Capt or Adjutant type told me to halt the men and come back with him to "see the Brigadier". Causing a little chaos in the traffic the men halted and we doubled back to the Brigadier, wondering what the devil was wrong. By then there was a queue of traffic, things having to slow up to pass our chaps who occupied a fair part of the road. People were staring down from the top of buses. The three of us stood on the pavement and the following conversation took place:–

Brig.   Your unit?
Me   8th Bn East Yorks, sir.
Brig.   Your C.O.?
Me   Lt. Col. E.B. Robinson, sir.
Brig.   How long have you been an N.C.O.?

Me	Since this morning, sir.
Brig.	Do you know an N.C.O. has to set an example?
Me	I don't quite follow what you mean. I am on my way to beach defences with a fatigue party.
Brig.	I did not ask you where you were going.
Me	If you have a complaint then I do not understand what it is.
Brig.	Listen to me corporal. (Dare I correct him, Lance Corporal, Brigadier please). I do not want to see you marching behind your men again. How do you lead someone from behind, eh? Tell me. You lead only in front and don't you forget that. Your men follow you.
Me	Yes, sir.
Brig.	Well off with you – there's a traffic queue through your squad.

The only redeeming thing about this horrible episode with everyone watching was the makings of a half wink and smile from the other bod who said nothing.

1st November 1940: transferred to "D" Company and to Horden, further south. Packing stores, etc. all day.

2nd November 1940: moved to Drill Hall, Horden. Some heating at last. They say the coal seam at the pit goes out to sea for three miles.

3rd November 1940: had to lay a cable to beach O.P. Very cold and wet. Getting an awful cold.

5th November 1940: went to chemist's for a bottle to avoid going on sick list. Little shop but very busy so I hung about until I could have a word with the chemist. I must have looked and sounded awful as he very kindly gave me a strong glass of quinine to be going on with plus a bottle. He asked where I came from and if I would like to come down to his house some evening for supper and a bath. Sounds a real treat as I don't like the time limit put on a bath when we marched to the pit head baths yesterday.

12th November 1940: called at the chemist's again hoping he would remember me and would ask me out. This was lucky because he reminded me he had said I had to look in again in about a week but the prospect of a civilian bath and a civilised supper must have made me forget or else I was deaf with the cold. I had to go to supper tonight. He and his wife walked back with me to the Drill Hall with their little Scottie. They have more than one shop in these parts and said if I could manage a Saturday off I could go for a run round in their car. They could not be kinder people and I've never felt so happy about a rotten cold. They call him Bob Johnson and his wife Jennie.

15th November 1940: whole company on a foul cross country run. Included one slag heap. We all cut ourselves on wire and with falls. Three miles in all. Boots and P.T. kit only. Came in first twenty.

18th November 1940: on guard at beach post. Horrible. Wet and muddy. Had to release pigeons at first light with a message tied to leg. Same message on both pigeons. This was to give wind direction for intelligence – gas warning. The code to use was "simplex towards" or "simplex against". What no-one told me was not to free the birds in fog or in sea mist. They just fluttered to the earth mound at the top of the post and sat there. Phoned HQ and told to recover them and send off later in clearer weather which we did. They circled round three times and then off to Wynyard Park, Brigade H.Q.

25th November 1940: letter from home. Enid very ill. Guard at beach post again. Still as wet and muddy though more boards down this time. Bitterly cold wind from the sea. Nothing to report.

10th December 1940: had some pleasant evenings with Mr. and Mrs. Johnson. Spam and chips for supper – a rare treat. Jennie darned some socks for me. Moved to Bn HQ at Seaburn today. Must see about a pass out to get to Horden.

27th December 1940: on guard duty Christmas Eve and went to Horden Boxing Day. Had a sleep in the morning. Lovely day. Mr. and Mrs. Whitfield saw me to the bus.

28th December 1940: assembled in the park in the morning to practice a Company attack. Capt Shackleton is a perfectionist and we had to stay out in the snow and do it all again. Our platoon got lost and failed to be where we were expected at the crucial time. Old Shack seemed to know where we were as he crept up behind us and threw some thunder flashes at us and said we were all dead.

29th December 1940: moved to the old eye hospital Roker today. "B" Coy 11 platoon. New Sgt. Major arrived today. Hell, what a man. Can't speak the King's English. Another one full of medal ribbons. Dare not move an eyelid on parade. Has been in umpteen campaigns and makes it quite clear he has no mercy in his soul for what he calls civilian soldiers. Has a voice like a bull and you can hear him miles away. Rumour has it he saved many lives at Dunkirk. The Lord grant us a leave or at least a pass out.

31st December 1940: what a way to spend a New Year's Eve. Fire picket in the docks. Nasty place with stacks of timber all over the place. No raid.

8th January 1941: several of platoon in detention for late returns. Mainly chaps from Hull whose homes had been hit and some bereaved. Standing orders now say air raids no excuse for late returns. You have to come back on time and then apply for compassionate leave.

[*Undated*:] Had some lovely weekends with Bob and Jennie and round the shops with Mr. and Mrs. Whitfield. I help load and unload various stocks for the shops at Coxhoe and Thornley. Mr.

and Mrs. Whitfield took me to the pictures in Horden and saw me on the last bus. I shall never meet kinder people.

16th February 1941: wireless telegraphy course in Seaburn. New sets to learn.

18th February 1941: mobile exercise with new sets. Went to Whitburn.

21st February 1941: "Scruff" Foster the new Sgt Major says we are getting soft with too many lectures so had us on a daddy of a route march today. Fifteen miles.

27th February 1941: C.O. came to watch us on a mobile exercise and said he was very pleased.

16th March 1941: moved to Leyburn, North Yorks to 10 Corps Junior Leaders School. This is for six weeks. Right out in the wilds.

23rd March 1941: if the remaining five weeks are like the last one we shall be fagged out. No place to go after lectures. Some night activity to come we are told. We all seem tired anyway.

[*Undated*:] Mobile exercises. Working with some Royal Corps of Signals whose standard is higher to give us practice at faster morse speeds. Lectures on tactics. Nothing special to note except jolly hard work at the time.

10th April 1941: tests in morse, field telephone, wireless and tactics. Passed them all except I got some of the wireless questions wrong.

14th April 1941: night exercises for two nights – not too bad.

25th April 1941: out of the passes only five got a Q1 and I was one of them. This means we cannot be re-classified for five years. Day off and packing up.

26th April 1941: returned to Sunderland. All personnel called out in the middle of the night and taken by transport to cliff top the other side of Whitburn where a destroyer had gone aground. What a job getting down the cliff in the dark. Hot cocoa arrived before first light and then had to man the beaches part of the time with Brens and take turns at unloading the shells from destroyer. A case of trying to beat the tide. Stood for long stretches in icy water and came out when nearly to waist. We stood in line, alternate facing to pass the shells down the line. The Doc came to examine our wrists and quite a lot had to fall out. The shells were very heavy and I saw some marked "gas". On the second inspection my wrists were swollen and I had to fall out. The destroyer was said to be part of an escort out of the Tyne and had made a navigational error. That was all we were told but it was awful to see such a fine ship out of action at a time when every destroyer was so precious.

27th April 1941: all unit assembled for security talk. Had not to answer any questions put to us by public about the destroyer. George Foster and I had already been asked by a couple of workmen on a bus as to what was "going on" down on the beach near Whitburn. We had said so far as we knew some other unit was making extra beach posts but it was not very convincing and they clearly did not believe us.

4th May 1941: large exercise started today. Called "Perce", and takes place over whole of Northumberland. The situation given to us was that the Tyne basin had been successfully invaded (steel helmets) and we (soft caps) had to repel the invaders.

10th May 1941: have lived rough for six nights in and around Rothbury – a lovely area. Awful casualties in this exercise. In a field not far from us some tanks pulled in for the night and ran over some chaps sleeping near a ditch at the side of the field. We had one jeep badly smashed but no-one hurt.

In trouble on the last day as the Intelligence Officer caught George Foster and I listening to Billy Cotton on BBC 6.2 m. latish on and we were not quick enough in flicking the frequency back to the unit frequency. He put a flash bomb under the P.U., took our names and unit and said we were dead. He had obviously been listening himself outside the truck.

11th May 1941: morning lecture on criticisms of the exercise etc. and the unfortunate episode of our listening to dance music and not on proper frequency was mentioned and we got a black mark. It was no use saying we would not do that in the real thing – this was supposed to be as near the real thing as could be managed with one proviso that we had not to damage the stone walls etc. We were also in trouble because we did not cross the river quickly enough. I was with the signals officer and waiting to cross the bridge when an umpire came up and said the bridge had just been bombed and was down. Col. Robinson heard this with obvious delight and made us all cross the river with as much gear as we could carry. It was icy cold and the old man stood on the bridge shouting the odds. Luckily the water was not too deep.

12th May 1941: moved to Hutton Rudby. Billet in a lovely little house in village square.

14th May 1941: field work and route march.

21st May 1941: Mr. and Mrs. Whitfield and Bob and Jennie came to see me and had a picnic. Lovely day. Very kind of them because petrol is rationed and there is little for pleasure use.

[*Undated*:] Nothing of note for some weeks. All field work, route marches and set pieces. We all seem bored with everything.

15th July 1941: C.O. got it into his head we ought to have a fell race and went to Great Ayton. This was a mile on the flat, up the feature and collect a ticket to prove it, down again a different way and a mile on the flat. This he said was to improve initiative. He brought the Doc out to examine each one. C.O.

we think is quite mad now. Said he used to do fell racing before breakfast when he was in India. I came tenth and enjoyed it.

1st August 1941: moved to West Hartlepool. Return to beach defences.

3rd August 1941: had to mount guard in public. Quite a crowd assembled. We can do this immaculately now like old soldiers as it were and I was "stick man" for the first time ever. One more body mounts guard than is required and on this occasion the extra was a NCO. The "stick man" is the runner for the guard and brings the supper etc., but the benefit is that there is a full night's sleep. When the order came for the stick man to fall out, it was awful marching across the huge area all alone but not without some satisfaction.

8th August 1941: managed a pass for the evening and went to Mr. and Mrs. Whitfield.

[*Undated*:] Had some hard route marches and guards near Seaton. Embarrassing time at the Whitfields. When I got there Mary wanted to take me to the pictures in West Hartlepool. I had nowhere near enough money on me and could hardly ask in front of everyone who was paying or that I did not want to go. She seems to have had some sort of tiff with Jack – I could sense something was wrong. Anyway we went in the car and Mary paid thank God. It was grand.

23rd November 1941: cold and wet. Moved to Middlesbrough. No-one seems to know what this move is for. We have no special job.

29th December 1941: sent for from home. Enid very ill. Granted 48 hours leave.

30th December 1941: sat up all night with Enid to let Mother and Father get some sleep. She is desperately ill as asthma followed the double pneumonia. I don't think she really knew who I was some of the time. The Doctor says she is very strong.

31st December 1941: told unit was moving to Chester so I reported there. Message received only just in time before I was setting off for Middlesbrough. Out of the blue some units in the 46th Division to have Bofors 40 mm training and we are one of them. We remain in the East Yorks for now but will go to Royal Artillery later. This means we shall be trained for two jobs which no-one likes. Any job must be better than the infantry and we've seen nothing yet but this alters the odds. We shall see.

[*Undated*:] All January and February lectures by the score, drills, foot and gun, tests, mobile exercises. We've done everything but fire the guns. In trouble few nights ago for walking across the holy of holies – the barrack square. It was foggy and George and I thought we would try a short cut to the billet but the RSM who was on the prowl heard us and a bull-like roar came across "Stand still those men". The bounder found us too despite the visibility and tore us off a strip making us walk the whole way round.

24th February 1942: advanced training and firing practice at Carnforth and Cark in Cartmel, Lancs. Right out in the wilds. What a dump. Instead of P.T. we have to have a run on the beach most mornings. Awful going in boots on the sands. The one today was two miles in all and came ninth.

28th February 1942: the whole day doing practice drills with semi-mobile bofors for ground targets, fire orders etc.

10th March 1942: practice firing with each person changing duties throughout the crew so we could all do each job under firing conditions.

24th March 1942: moved to Dover on coastal defences. Saw

some small convoys in the Channel, fairly close in but being shelled from France. No hits but some very close to some of the ships. They all sailed merrily on and never altered course even. Had to clear out of our Nissen huts every time the big gun fired in St. Margaret's Bay. Awful row. This gun shells enemy shipping and can reach the coast of France.

7th April 1942: sent to Hoo, Nr. Chatham on an aircraft recognition course for three weeks. Not a bad spot. Passed the course.

28th April 1942: moved to Ashford, Kent. Had a 21 mile route march in FSMO (Field Service Marching Order). Bad one this and some feet casualties, mine included. Never had any bother until now. Doctor and two nurses came round and I had both heels cut off and cannot walk. Right round the perimeter of both. I have a piggy back to the mess and cannot go out.

[Undated:] Wish they would make their minds up what we are supposed to be doing. Revision of infantry work now. Current affairs lectures.

10th May 1942: feet nearly healed. Moved to Lille Barracks Folkestone. Place almost dead and could get nowhere near the beaches for the defences. More lectures and practice situations. Some FW 190 came in from the sea (with the sun in our eyes) and some damage done in Folkestone. No sign of our own equipment yet but some vehicles have arrived for us.

28th May 1942: more revision and lectures. Smallish route march gave no further bother to heels. Our C.O. seems convinced our role on Bofors is for a limited spell and seems to take delight in going over everything again and again. We can do two jobs now very thoroughly. Wish the equipment would arrive and then we would know where we stand.

18th July 1942: moved in convoy to Butlin's Camp Clacton-on-

Sea, Essex. Started early and it was a bad convoy. Before we were through London I got separated and found myself leading about ten vehicles. The despatch riders who are the sheep dogs of a convoy just could not keep us all together. Military police were to take us through London but they only took the first section. We managed somehow and when clear of London and trying to catch up we had an accident. When we came to a "steep hill" sign we seemed to be going very fast, towing a two-ton Bofors and I said to George had he not better change gear or slow up or something but he had not seen the sign alas and we accelerated alarmingly over the crest of the hill. The cab of a Bedford QL is closed so we could not communicate with the toggle rope man but Noble having the good sense to feel something was wrong, hanked on the rope and locked the wheels. There was a bend at the bottom of the hill and with a horrible screech of tyres in an attempt to take the bend on our correct side we were horrified to see the muzzle of a field gun sticking out of the corner. There ought to have been a chap on duty opposite – a strict convoy rule when vehicles stop but no-one was there. It was another convoy stopped in front of us. Only one thing was left so as to avoid the muzzle going straight through our radiator and causing an almighty mess and that was not to take the corner at all and hope nothing was coming in the opposite direction. This we did and crashed straight through railings and gate, right across a vegetable garden and landed with the lorry radiator literally touching the front door of a cottage.

The occupants were not about yet and came to the window in night attire. They were angry as this was the third time in five months a military vehicle had destroyed their garden and gate. By then Lt. Sayer had come back and after a few words with the householders, took measurements of the skid marks. The lorry had to use four wheel drive to get out of the garden and we pushed the gun out. We then travelled along to Clacton, the rest of the convoy moving on. We are bound to be in trouble about this one.

20th July 1942: practice shooting most of the day. At a sleeve towed by an Anson. Never hit anything but a few plus shots. Not good enough according to the old man.

28th July 1942: returned to Shorncliffe Barracks, Folkestone. Had a short hit and run air raid. Some damage, no casualties.

30th July 1942: arrived in Stubbington, Hants. Final tests on Bofors and mobile exercises.

12th August 1942: returned to Folkestone. Coastal defence and guards.

21st August 1942: arrived Ashford to be fitted with new equipment.

3rd September 1942: the war is three years old today. I suppose we are lucky to be in England still. World wide the news is not good and there seems no end to it all. David Ashton shot down in a Wellington over Heligoland – killed. Eric Wright shot down in a Hurricane in the Battle of Britain now two years in the past. Fred Garnett in the bag somewhere, caught in Crete. Something to be thankful for. We had a long discussion tonight about what exactly we had achieved in three years. We came to the conclusion that few units must have walked or run as far, done as many guards, had to change from one complete role in the Army to another one. We have shot at a few aircraft and not hit anything, been in a few air raids and kept ourselves fit. That about summed it up.

5th September 1942: arrived in Hythe at first operational site with new Bofors. Fully manned all day and guard at night. Only saw one Focke Wulf fighter early one morning. Came in low from the sea with the sun in our eyes. Dropped two bombs, circled round by which time we had the right deflection and he hopped it unscathed.

17th September 1942: relieved from site and return to Clacton-on-Sea.

23rd September 1942: had to perform in front of a lot of top brass with the Stifkey Stick sight. Our lot hit a lot of sleeves and were complimented. This sight is on the secret list. Jolly clever gadget provided the plane does not exceed 500 mph which none do yet.

6th October 1942: glad to be away from Clacton. Cold miserable place. Returned to Ashford and handed in all equipment after tests, revision, exercises, route marches, lectures ad infinitum.

4th December 1942: train to Aldershot. We were told today the camp would be visited by a "very important person" and there was speculation if it was to be Mr. Churchill or Mr. Eden but it was the King. We were all bulled up and he walked between all the ranks. He looked pale and heavily made up. He looked each one of us in the face. He never said where we were going or when but wished us all well. Told us we would be having some leave in a few days and no guard duties at which everyone laughed. Too good to be true.

14th December 1942: kit checks galore. New clothes issued. Rumour of leave.

15th December 1942: home embarkation leave. Train from King's Cross packed like sardines. Stood nearly all the way. Managed a seat at Doncaster. Mother and Father could not do enough for me and it was sad to see how Enid's illness seems to have worn them down. On Sunday morning we could not all go to church together so Father and I went early and walked across the Knavesmire and heard the POWs singing. They are in the race-course stands.

18th December 1942: Father and Blagdon came to the station to see me off to King's Cross. Mother and Enid walked from the back of the house in Pulleyn Drive to the railway cutting to wave. It was a brave effort on her sticks and must have taken a lot out of her. The train was packed and I just managed to get to the window to wave a large handkerchief as directed. I wonder if they saw me as bodies seemed to be hanging out of every window. I stood in the corridor a while looking at the familiar fields and villages to try and stop myself getting all mixed up. There seemed to be something special about coming away this time. All the other times I had just left the house and said "cheerio" knowing that I might have a few days at home in a few more months and so on. Now that was finished. Alamein has cheered everyone up but the papers say it is only the beginning. If ever there was a time when one ought to be allowed to lift the veil as it were and peep round the corner, this is it, I thought. Enid looked so ill I began to wonder if I would see her again, then the family. Then the horrible thought was that it might be me who was not going to come back and at that, feeling reasonably in low spirits I fought my way back to my seat and fell asleep just after Selby.

20th December 1942: more kit inspections. Some lectures on current affairs. Later it was every man for himself to the nearest tavern. On return Capt Davies and Lt Brown asked all the Sgts to the Officers' Mess for a wee drop. Final roll call. As names called out we all stepped in to a large shed opposite the parade ground and formed up ready to march to the station. The C.O. gave us a pep talk, never said where we were going, and the RSM for once smiled and took a paternal interest in us all. Laden to the hilt we marched off in bright moonlight to the station. The silhouettes of the buildings and the gaze of the odd late passer-by stuck in my memory. We entrained six to a compartment with full kit and settled down to sleep as best we could. So began a journey to some foreign part – we did not even know the embarkation port when we entrained at Aldershot.

23rd December 1942: arrived at Liverpool King George Dock in the small hours. Lt Todd grabbed me for a baggage party so I had to stay behind and all the others boarded trams lined up and ready to go to the docks. We went in transport and on arrival at the docks Lt Todd had miraculously disappeared as he has the habit of doing and I found myself landed with the whole baggage and no-one to ask and no idea of where it should be dumped.

None of the drivers knew anything and I was quite lost. Other units were about waiting to embark. The only reference was our convoy number painted on kit bags and by reference to this I found the rest of the unit under NO. 34575 waiting to embark. Tea was on the go and the baggage party disappeared. I was then told I had put all the baggage near the wrong gang plank so had to find another baggage party. I was then told to get more men because the whole lot had to be embarked in one go. There was to be no running up and down the gang plank. The Military police made this quite clear because of a final check of names. What a mess. No breakfast.

The ship was not very attractive. Called HMT *Derbyshire* 12,000 tons and a peace time trooper for 1500 men. Our whole Brigade of about 3,000 were embarking on it. Little did we know the inconvenience in store for us. There was a multitude of things going on all round us at the dock side and we stood and watched it all, completely bewildered. The mess deck to which we were allocated will leave a lasting impression on me. I slung a hammock with a couple of hundred others on 'F' deck. Very hot and could not sleep properly. Did not know until later it was below the water line.

24th December 1942: up early, tired out. Horrible breakfast. Sure there are too many of us on this ship. Still in dock. Wandered around to get bearings. A and B decks are out of bounds to all ranks so we went looking for a place to sleep in the open if need be on C deck but there was little spare going. Decided not to go back to F deck.

Pulled out into the estuary mid-morning amid cheers, waves and signs from the dockers. Also rude songs from the ship. All very moving. Lay a few miles out. Saw a smallish aircraft carrier being towed in with all its rear blown in. A rude reminder at an unfortunate time since we had not even started the journey yet.

PART TWO: NORTH AFRICA

25 December 1942 to 6 September 1943

25th December 1942: set sail in a northerly direction with four other ships who had joined us in the night. They look like troopers. Only two escorting Destroyers so far. At mid-day one of the Destroyers came very close and displaced a notice "Merry Christmas" to which there were cat calls, boos and cheers. Read a lamp signal from leading Destroyer telling the other ships to keep in single line until reaching main body of the convoy. The pilot seemed to be with us a long time and he waved as he pulled away from us. The last English civilian we could see for a long time perhaps.

It was a lovely morning, a little sun, bitterly cold wind and racing white clouds. Few could resist the temptation to keep looking back at the Liverpool skyline, now just a greyish blob on the horizon. Stood for long periods watching the other ships and the destroyers. We talked of happier Christmas Days.

The Journey: nothing to do but settle down to make the best of what is to me an awe-inspiring situation. A little frightening sometimes. Herded about all day and gradually getting to know the way around. Food the worst I have ever had and Christmas Dinner a real disgrace. Awful row about it all over the boat. Rumour has it we are going to the North of Scotland to collect some more ships for the convoy. We are all hoping there will be more than four destroyers anyway. F deck is no good for sleeping. Do not like being below water level and an awful smell below decks. Left my hammock after last night and a party of us found a spot on D deck. Cold but better than below.

George Ounsley not well. Regular boat drills and tests for putting on our kapok floats. Instructions for wearing of gym shoes at certain times, unit by unit, instead of boots to cut down noise. Regular P.T. unit by unit around the decks. On the second day out met a large ship *"The Empress of Australia"*. Along with a few others from the Clyde we now make nine ships in all. There is an escort of seven destroyers, two Corvettes and a couple of Hudson aircraft today. Very comforting but wonder how long the aircraft will stay.

We went round the top of N. Ireland and started to zig zag all the time. None of the crew would say very much if you could get hold of one for a chat. No-one was allowed on A or B decks but we asked about the constant changing of course and were told that every seven minutes for the whole of the journey this would take place, day and night. This impressed us as a remarkable feat of navigation and timing especially in the night as we are all fairly close. This morning there was a race to the side of the boat to see where we had taken up our position and found that whereas at last light we were in the middle of the middle line, now we were like tail end Charlie, right on the outside at the back. How we managed this in the night must remain a mystery. Told we are doing 12 knots by day and 16 knots at night. Must be an old tub this one because it groans and rattles in the night but not in the day time when not going so fast.

The Atlantic looks very grey and uninviting. Endless sea. Although I suppose no-one is enjoying this one cannot escape a feeling of pride at these little destroyers. A comfort and boost to morale in fact. More boat drills and fitting of floats. The toilets are not working properly and we are inspected every day to make sure we are free from infection and bugs.

I clicked for S.O.S. (Ship's Orderly Sgt) today and must have walked miles. I certainly know my way around now and do not take the wrong turnings so often. Quite a swell today but one of the crew said the conditions were noted in the ship's log as "choppy". To us it seems rough never mind choppy because now and again we can see the propeller of the ship in front come right out of the water. We are doing this because the whole ship shudders when the propeller is out. Now the washing facilities have packed up as well as the toilets.

George Ounsley lost top and bottom set of teeth this morning. I was with him lying down in C deck lounge and the boat was heaving first one way and then the other. Awful but never felt sick. George was almost green. Have never seen anyone his colour before. The deck was hot and stuffy so I suggested we better have some air and went outside. All the time he was trying to vomit but could not do so. By the time we got to a spare space on the rails, loads more were vomiting over the side, George was in a bad way and he made a weird noise, bent over the side and away they went – top and bottom set to the deeps of the Atlantic. We have no bread on board so poor old George has to have everything sloppy to be able to eat. More boat drills.

Cliff Raine and I had some requests played for us at last over the radio. Ours came just at twilight and we had the Warsaw Concerto for about the twentieth time the last few days. We had a last cigarette before it was time for no smoking above decks. Clear night. Saw each ship signal to the one opposite giving the conditions of its black-out precautions. The trash goes over at night time too.

We still have no idea where we are going but rumour has it we are still heading out into the Atlantic. We have seen no sun to help with any clues. So many are sick and poorly on the boat there is bags of grub all of a sudden. Have felt O.K. so far.

Had our first genuine scare today, 30th December, when sirens went and we stood at boat stations. It was just before last light. The action was on our side and we saw two destroyers detach themselves and race ahead, dropping several depth charges. They turned quickly and dropped more then went on again. We all increased speed and the leader fell back nearer the front of the convoy. Then the two destroyers came back and took up their places again. We were stood down in about 45 minutes. I did not like just standing there in the dark waiting for the all clear.

Today is New Year's Eve and we were told we were bound

for Algiers as reinforcements for the First Army, presently held up in Tunisia and furthermore, we would be passing through the Straits of Gibraltar at about midnight. That is all we were told. We are all going to stay up for the New Year. Went on deck about 2350 hours and to our horror found we were all alone. Rest of the convoy disappeared and we were going at a devil of a speed. Just could not see any other boat or the escort and it was a clear night.

Then we saw the lights of the Moroccan coast and knew we were about either through or opposite the Rock. Drunk each other's health with water and tried to sleep. At first light we were all together again and the first job was to count the escort and ourselves. It was then given off that the convoy split up to go through the Straits, went maximum speed and formed up again inside and that we had all been together since about 1 a.m. How do the Navy do it.

1st January 1943: greeted today by some large units of the Mediterranean Fleet. We were told one was HMS *Renown* and a Carrier *Formidable*. They were a very impressive sight with their escorts of what looked like Cruisers and Destroyers. This part of the Fleet led us in to Algiers. The sight of Algiers from the sea was a wonderful one and I shall never forget it. There were large Mosques and white flat topped buildings which stood out against a background of brown and green hills. Had a long wait to disembark and when we did it was on to a floating dock. Very glad to leave the "*Altmark*" as the trooper had been christened.

With full kit, we lined up on the dock and set off to walk one of the Sgt Major's "half miles" to a place where large kit bags were dumped with valises. This left us in FSMO (Field Service Marching Order) and we fell out. Some of us regretted soft shoes had to be worn for so long on the boat as we were obviously in for a long march. No vehicles in sight.

Something went radically wrong with the operations tonight. Either the maps were wrong or we had set off on the wrong road in the first place. Word came down the line that we only had to walk five miles to a place called Maison Caree and this was a piece of cake in the cool of the evening but when we had done 16 kilometres – about ten miles – word came down the line we only had another three to do. Rain came with considerable force which changed the mood somewhat. We saw no other troops and were beginning to feel the march now so that after a halt it was agony to start again. At well after midnight, weary, hungry and drenched even with capes that we halted again and were told we were nowhere near our destination. Two men dropped out at 1 a.m. and were left and by now we had done nearly twenty miles. Each one had to have a share of the Bren gun. A final stop at 2 a.m. and we were told we had three kilometres to go. The last stretch was done in complete silence as we were about all in.

At last we arrived and our sleeping quarters were an old wine cellar minus any wine and after raiding a nearby barn for all the straw we could get, were soon asleep. After only four hours' sleep instructions were issued that each man could use his tablet for making a warm drink for breakfast which was hard biscuits and bully beef. Each of us carries 48 hours rations. Tinned cheese, sweets, chocolate and bully beef. Lecture on a few points about Arab men and their women folk as it seems we may be allowed out. The Arab woman is always accompanied by her husband. We were warned that any rude remarks about the man being on the pony or donkey and the woman often loaded with wares etc. walking behind might end in trouble. Told not to stare at the Arab women.

5th January 1943: heard today that our rear party on a separate convoy leaving after us was torpedoed before the run in to Gibraltar. No lives lost but all our gear and transport gone. Feet still sore but managed a couple of miles to the village of Baraki for some wine and to get accustomed to the new currency.

12th January 1943: told this morning we were likely to move up to the front area in a few days and will take over fresh gear and guns there. Went to Baraki again tonight and had a lot of Grand Via Rouge wine. Horrible stuff.

14th January 1943: half a day off for everyone and went to Algiers. The beauty we had seen from the sea soon vanished. A dirty smelly place and troops at present only allowed there in daylight. The Casbah and market were interesting and we wandered round the shopping centre. Had a meal in an hotel and went to the pictures. We had a feeling all the time we were not welcome.

16th January 1943: assembled early in a massive convoy. Impressive sight. Followed the only route to Tunisia – about 500 miles – carrying all our own petrol and food.

End of convoy: journey took over three days. Went through Constantine and Souhk areas to Ghardimaou just outside the Tunisian border. All very barren and a true wilderness but beautiful in the mountains. One day we did 6 miles in bottom gear and one moment would be freezing on the top of a mountain and an hour later too warm in the valley below. This was between Souhk Areas and Ghardimaou. Before the mountains started we halted for the night and slept by our vehicles. There were double guards on duty. I slept next to Sgt Vipond and we had for pillows our small packs. When we woke he pulled my leg because his pack was missing. Then other things were discovered as missing including some weapons. The natives had stolen up on us and had a free for all along the wagon lines. There was an awful row about this and we realised how new we were to soldiering. Weapons chained the next night.

The final stop for checking stores, vehicle maintenance etc., was outside Ghardimaou. Here we saw an Arab funeral. Everyone was wailing and singing songs. All dressed in bright colours. Robes of red and blue and walked in a straggling line towards a hillside not far from where we were and where a rough grave had been dug. All the Arabs stood round the grave whilst the body was tossed up quite high in a sheet. The belief is that if the body falls to the grave face upwards, the soul has gone to Heaven and if face down, gone to Hell. We could not see the result from where we were but the gathering soon dispersed to more wailing as in single file they walked back down the hill.

20th January 1943: preparations now complete and a final talk by our C.O. saw the end of our stay in Algeria. Moved near Tabarka where we had our first deployment just inside the Tunisian border. The V.P. (Vulnerable Point) was a bridge. We were told the enemy had tried several times to destroy the bridge. Last night we all slept in a farm yard and on straw and today everyone is itching badly. Sent the men down two at a time to a little stream to wash. Thirty bugs according to Borrill came out of his socks. Had some de-lousing powder sent up and this did the trick. You could see the bugs jump off when the powder was put on.

22nd January 1943: Bob Goodrum bought or stole a hen today. He said he paid 60 fr for it but no-one believes him. Bought or stolen, it laid two eggs this morning which we all thought a remarkable feat. To make sure it does not escape there is a long piece of string attached to it and it is well fed. Although we have not tasted what war is all about yet we are beginning to develop that awful feeling when you almost know that at any time something can happen and we began in a way to envy this hen who must know nothing about our privations, bugs or why we are here. It is well fed. A complete achievement and success. Mounsey threatened to kill and eat it if it did not accelerate production. We like the old bird.

24th January 1943: orders came today to move to a deployment round 277 Bty of the 70th Field Regt R.A. They have twenty-five pounders and are at Sejanane. Due to heavy rains it was not possible to make the required position so we had to take an alternative route on the edge of a wood some way from the V.P.

25th January 1943: bombed and machine gunned at first light this morning. No warning and barely time to get the gun into action. There were eleven ME 109s and I saw a couple of FW 190. It seemed all over in under a minute. Not very pleasant. No casualties either with us or the Field Regt. They all came in straight from the sea with the look-out giving the alarm when they were almost on us. We must be well camouflaged as the bombs were all over the place. There is not a lot of difference between an ME 109 and a Spitfire unless you get them head on but the look-out should have alarmed us at the sound of aircraft anyway.

[*Undated*:] Moved to fresh site and took two hours to winch gun out of position. Finished at 3 a.m. in new site near the original one intended. Had a tot of whisky and a biscuit with Capt Davies. Very cold and muddy. Awfully tired and we haven't really started yet.

[*Undated*:] Moved again to a "hide-out" in Happy Valley from which we deployed to protect a .55 Medium Gun. Bitterly cold, hail and rain. Mud everywhere. Woke up to find ourselves straight in front of "Greenhill" and "Baldy". These are two formidable features dominating the valley and where the 1st Army had had to stop in its initial push in to Tunisia. We are under canvas behind a ridge and out of observation from the two features. A tragedy happened this morning when two Hurricanes came over. We stood to on the sound of aircraft and Borrill shouted "They're ours" when we were amazed to see them swoop down at our rear and let loose what would be 250 pounders. We were told later they had bombed our own Brigade HQ, destroying some vehicles and injured the Padre who might have to lose one of his legs. He has gone out and we hope can be flown back to hospital. The blame was put on incorrect French maps but a pilot must have a difficult job in country like this and at speed.

27th January 1943: had some engagements today but did not hit anything. Not bad shooting though. ME 109s. Borrill covered the rear with a Bren and with every third round being tracer says he saw some go in to the tail of one plane but they all cleared off without sign of difficulty.

29th January 1943: month since we left Blighty and no mail yet. Orders came to move to the original V.P. in forward area to protect some light Field Artillery. The place is called "The Ridge". The gun had to be dug in to avoid observation so we had to do this in the dark. No movement in daylight on the ridge. Field guns deployed on lower slopes of Ridge behind us and all heavily camouflaged. Atrocious weather. No Man's Land in front of us for about 1500 yards to the base of "Greenhill" and "Baldy". The 25 pounders use the tip of these features a lot to get the O.P. (Observation Post). The whole of the ridge is shelled frequently so the Bosche knows we are here.

30th January 1943: went to see Capt Douglas the Bty Commander of the 78th Field Regt to find out any gen or news and when I was nearly down the ridge alone a heavy barrage started so I flung myself down at the edge of one of the guns only to get the netting tangled round the buttons of my greatcoat. I wriggled to try and extricate myself but that only made matters worse. I had one desire and that was to get down the first hole I could find. There were yells from all quarters to get out of it and so on but the more I tried the worse the tangle became. I then tried to undo all the buttons but this was also difficult in a lying position and I seemed to be firmly in the netting so I lay there until the shelling stopped which seemed like an eternity. Two gunners came out and with their help I was freed and we dashed to a slit trench in case the shelling started again. The ones with the horrible screech are near ones. The one you don't hear is the end of everything. No guns were hit but the range was spot on and there were several near misses. Our chaps are alright further up the ridge but it is a weird feeling wondering when it is all going to start again.

2nd February 1943: no relief from terrible weather conditions. If we have to get out of here in a hurry we shall never do it with equipment. Made our first "kill" today and reported it officially with the support of a witness from the gunners. It was last light and an ME 109 all alone was having a look around so we had a go and got his fin and rudder. The plane dived steeply and the pilot baled out. I think he would have dropped in our forward positions. I ordered a cease fire and not to machine gun the pilot as Wilmot was shouting to do. The others thought he would drop in German lines and that this made it different. All the terrible things happening at sea were quoted to me as a reason why the pilot should have been shot at and they said I was soft and so on. Wilmot, whose home had been wiped out in Hull, was most vehement. I'm sure it was the right thing to do though. The chaps feel very strongly about it.

Went to see Capt Douglas about the official hit and he said he would also report it. He also said I did the correct thing in not shooting at the pilot who in his opinion would now be a prisoner in our lines. Capt Douglas said he may have been taking photographs of the Ridge and congratulated us on a good bit of shooting. Capt Douglas goes out some evenings to our O.P. which is to the side and round "Greenhill" and he told me about his last operation where he noticed at first light a lot of movement and then a large parade forming up as if it was a breakfast queue or something. He waited until he thought a maximum number of men were paraded and instead of getting a ranging shot from his battery as would normally be the case he took a chance on the range and ordered a Bty target on this open space of ground. The range was accurate and shells fell in and around the whole parade. The casualties must have been enormous. Crouched in a confined space, facing the sun where the slightest glint would have been seen, Capt Douglas spent the rest of the day and the whole of the hillside around his O.P. was plastered at regular intervals. He got out at night unscathed and said he would not use the same spot again. What a dirty business this all is. We came to the view in our discussions etc. that it has to be accepted in order to survive. I liked Capt Douglas. He was a bit like a young public school master and it was all part of a game and jolly good fun style. Has to be done old boy attitude. I reminded him of the pilot and he went to some pains to explain the difference in the situation.

[*Undated*:] Capt Davies came to inspect our defences in case the infantry had to withdraw. Told us the I.O. (Intelligence Officer) insisted our trenches faced the other way, i.e. opposite to the way we had dug them. I had made them facing the only obvious way of an attack but had to alter them and extend them. I still held the view that an attack could only come from the left flank. Heavy night activity with infantry patrols and incessant mortar fire. We began to feel a bit depressed as to how a way would ever be forced up the valley between "Greenhill" and "Baldy". Little sleep.

12th February 1943: heaviest shelling of the ridge yet. Bloody awful it was. No casualties with us. Two injured in the 25 pounders lower down.

14th February 1943: our 25 pounders had some targets today and were active. At last light the shelling started again. It seems only aircraft can put these guns out as it will have to be the long range ones from further back if there is to be no aircraft. The Field Regt we protect supports a full Brigade of infantry and must obviously be causing concern to the Germans. Tonight was the first time we have heard our own 25 pounders continuing with a target whilst enemy shelling was in progress. We could hear the orders being given on the tannoy system. Barrage went on for a long time.

18th February 1943: message from HQ this morning asking if we had seen a large Alsatian type dog answering to the name of "French". I replied that we saw it most nights following the same route through our lines, away to the left and along the valley to the left of "no man's land". Reply later came that this dog must be killed. It was a highly intelligent animal which had been known to lead German patrols into our lines and sometimes in the day strayed into our areas, returning to the German lines at night.

20th February 1943: all beginning to feel jumpy now. This shelling is beyond description and whilst we are on the slope the odd one has landed right on the ridge. Either we have been spotted or the odd shell is a healthy "minus" but the Germans obviously know the 25 pounders are in the dip. The gun flashes at night will be sufficient for that.

22nd February 1943: torrential rain. Heavy barrage at first light. What a start to the day. Ounsley is very cheerful. He keeps saying to everyone "not to worry, if there's one with your name on it there's nothing you can do about it" and with this rather carefree philosophy the spirit seems to rise but it seems the periods of quiet are just as bad. You begin to wonder when it will all start again. The dog appeared at last light today and Stoney took two quick pot shots at it and missed. Hope it comes back again but it was difficult to see at dusk.

23rd February 1943: new Padre came today. Had to bellow at him as he left his motor bike and calmly walked along the ridge, the clot. He moved lower down the ridge and asked me how many would like communion. Out of the detachment of twelve, four attended and it was very moving. He had a little suit case with a miniature communion plate set in it and a little stole. We moved over behind a bit of scrub but it was hard to concentrate. I don't think I shall ever forget the little service. Here in the midst of complete madness was a breath of peace but it was not like being in a proper church. "It is very meet, right and our bounden duty that we should at all times and in all places give thanks unto thee O Lord" and so on. It was hard to give thanks for anything though I suppose we were in one piece and that was something to be thankful for. This was the first time we had seen the new Padre. Nice chap and sincere. "Therefore with Angels and Archangels and with all the company of heaven we laud and magnify thy glorious name" and so it went on. After it was all over he had a general chat with the chaps and he went on his way.

24th February 1943: was asked over to the gunners to have some fried spam. The oven was a shell case dug in the side of a trench but it was a slow business creating the heat required because of smoke so we waited until dark and quite enjoyed it. Respite in the shelling – very suspicious.

25th February 1943: had a few hours sleep last night. Shelling started again at first light. Few hit the top of the ridge and some overshot the 25 pounders. No casualties but an unpleasant start to the day. Lt Brown came later in morning and told us of some casualties. One serious with a leg off and on his way back to Algiers. Others were gun shot wounds. No sign of mail. Heavy rain.

26th February 1943: Lt Brown came again. Two visits in two days – something is up. He said Intelligence had had a warning of an attack which was possible, estimated 500 strong, on our left flank. This was the very direction I had said in the first place but had been told to alter the position of our trenches. Lt Brown said we had to get the gun out of the pit and prepare for a ground shoot. One would have thought the Germans had heard him say this because the moment we started there was an awful stonk. We were all very tired when finished but the gun was raised, ammunition re-stacked and we were ready as ordered. I have the feeling we are all very scared. Once the shelling has started there is little you can do about it but it is the quiet periods between stonks, wondering when it will start again. The chaps are in good form with their banter, etc., but underneath it all everyone keeps talking about the one you don't hear. The shell travels more quickly than sound therefore you hear the swish or screech after the sickening thud in the soft earth on or near the ridge. When you don't hear the swish therefore you are dead in line and then in Kingdom Come. The argument is that this is an old soldier's tale but it isn't. Double guards.

27th February 1943: Capt Davies sent his "do or die" message this morning. This said we had not to move out of our present position. Help was coming. The infantry were likely to pull out at last light. The chaps were less than lukewarm when I told them help was on its way. Any major attack would surely be preceded by heavy shelling and as things had been quiet for a few hours I went to see Capt Douglas in the hope of getting some better intelligence since he had a radio and we had not.

He had no further news and I only just made it back to our lines when the shelling started again.

28th February 1943: double guards beginning to tell. No news and no help or fresh orders. Feel awfully tired. Went to see Capt Douglas again. He said he had just received orders to spike his guns and get out. I felt sad to hear this. A shell is reversed down the barrel and fired by remote control lanyard making the gun useless. He said he would find a few targets to get rid of the ammo first. Hurried back to the chaps and told them that with no news from HQ for 24 hours, coupled with the gunners getting out, we had two options. First to leave everything and get away from the ridge or stay put in accordance with the last message. This would mean either being killed or taken prisoner as it was obvious something big was afoot to get us out of the valley. I had just finished explaining the situation as I understood it when Capt Douglas sent a message to say that the Corps Cdr had instructed the valley be cleared and nothing was to move up it. The gunners were about to spike their guns and go. The time was about 10.30 a.m. There had been torrential rain which I hoped would postpone any attack and I said we would give it to noon. Rations will be finished in 48 hours and it could take us some time to find the unit. At about 10.45 a.m. we were bombed and shelled as never before. Had not seen any aircraft for a few days but these meant business – Stukas. They seemed to drop like stones out of nowhere. It would have been suicide to move anywhere so we lay low until it was all over. I think apart from getting on the boat at Liverpool when I prayed hard for a safe journey, today I experienced real fear for the first time. Or perhaps I had felt this before and not recognised it. What bothered me as well was the disobedience of the orders and having to justify whatever we decided to do.

Guard shouted to come to the top of the ridge. The time was 11 a.m. To my horror I saw through my glasses some small armoured cars moving slowly on a fixed line to the left where I knew there was an old rail track. This was rough country and the cars in single file never wavered so we presumed they had

To : No. 2 Det

FROM : THQ.

Sgt Hudson

It is do or die to-night. I am coming up with 3·Tonner · equipment and working party of approx 12 Men + Major ?? Have the Tractor ready to move off at approx 1830 6. don't move un til I arrive at your Wagon Lun.

The Tractor Must be completely unloaded will the exception of Vehicle Tools and Vehicle Equip.

You will leave 2 Men + 1 N.C.O on Guard over the kit you leave -the rest of the Detachment will be in Tractor ready to move off when I call.

P.S (1) Don't forget to take A. Barrel & Ammo. off
(2) Ensure Skid Chains are tight

The help which never came, Battle of the Ridge, Sedjenane, February 1943.

ORDER OF THE DAY

The following order of the day has been issued by General Alexander.

"Soldiers of the Allies. The enemy is making a desperate bid to break through the iron ring which is closing round him. [...] can finally overwhelm him. [...] defeat this hostile thrust as we must and will then his fate in TUNISIA is sealed. Stand firm. Fight and kill the enemy. A great Allied victory is within our grasp if every soldier does his duty.

Sg. H.R. ALEXANDER

In the Field
24th Feb, 43

General.
Commanding 18 Army Group.

Order of the Day, 24 February 1943.

the same wheel base as the track and were actually on the line. They peppered the top of the ridge with machine gun and small cannon. We had one Bren, some tommy guns and the Bofors 40 mm.

The angle of firing was very restricted because of the slope on the ridge and there was no time to move the gun so we put it to the best advantage to cover the only small arc possible. Everyone stood to and I sent a runner down the ridge to the track to try and find out what was happening as the front line seemed to have moved. He came back with the news that the York and Lancs were pulling out and the Leicesters were the rear-guard. It then became clear to me that if we did not move we would be trapped with little to defend ourselves. First we discharged a few boxes of ammo through the small arc in the hope of hitting something – our presence was obviously known so it did not matter. The gun sight known as the Stifkey Stick was still on the secret list so we destroyed it. We then fixed a Heath Robinson type of booby trap to one of the traversing handles of the gun but it looked so obvious we dismantled it and fixed a grenade under the platform so that any movement would pull out the pin. The barrel was removed, put in a trench muzzle up and two grenades rolled down. Amazing how far one can go in four seconds. Had no time to attend to the spare barrel but the gun was useless.

At noon with no news we decided to go but at that moment all hell seemed to be let loose at the ridge and we just had to freeze and wait until it was over. There were no casualties. Decided the order of moving from point to point along the ridge one at a time. We all assembled safely about half an hour later none the worse, in a ditch by the track. After a breather, a platoon of Leicesters came by and I asked how many were left. They said not many and advised we got out sharply.

The German advance down the left flank was keeping pace with the withdrawal because we were pasted at regular intervals as we started to move down the valley. What was the forward area got no shelling at all. After about an hour when we had covered I think not more than three miles, some heavy stuff started landing in front of us, dead on the track. It was now clearly obvious the

Germans knew we were moving out. We left the track and moved parallel to it. Two ME 109s just appeared from nowhere. We did not even hear them. We scattered and froze. They both strafed the track and missed us. The second one came round for another look and Borrill had by then loaded the Bren and started firing from a crouched position. It was excellent shooting (every third bullet a tracer) but he went off unharmed which was a relief in our present state.

The going was too rough off the track so we resumed on it after a breather and I was amazed to see a young Lt on a motor cycle coming from the rear. He stopped and asked who we were etc. I told him we had heard the valley was being cleared and that we were trying to find our unit. He said we had nine miles to go to Sedjenane. He then asked for a volunteer to go with him to lay some booby traps. Stoney became the hero of the moment as he volunteered and after dramatic goodbyes etc., the last we saw of him was clinging to the young Lt with a tatty old suitcase between him and the Lt.

We moved steadily down the valley in single file a few yards apart. Shells now started dropping both in front and behind. We just flung ourselves down anywhere and hoped for the best, being thankful that no more aircraft were about. The heat which followed the rain made us all thirsty and we did not have a lot of water but we stopped in a small wadi for a breather. It felt safe to be in the wadi – small and narrow away surely from any attention. We had one guard at each end. No sooner had we stretched out than Borrill shouted ME 109s. They swooped down and strafed the length of the wadi and again we escaped. How Borrill saw them I shall never know. He is a jolly good spotter. In anticipation of coming round a second time Borrill had the Bren ready with a mag on and whilst we were pressed hard to the wadi wall he lay as if he could not care less and emptied one of our last mags. Mercifully they did not return and again Borrill became the hero of the day.

Whilst being conscious of the fact that this was our first baptism I have to admit to being scared and only hoped it was not showing. I think we all feel the same. No-one talked very much. In the wadi I felt my tongue go dry, the palms of the hands cold, a quickening of the pulse and then breaking out in a sweat more than normal because of the heat.

Decided to cut the stop short and move from the wadi and back on the track. More aircraft were heard and to our delight they were three Spits who patrolled up and down the valley for a few minutes and disappeared.

Towards late afternoon the shelling was all to our rear and we came across some medium artillery in a wood. These were 55s. Sheltered in the wood – unwisely as things turned out. The Germans obviously knew of this artillery for there was the most terrific stonk. With plenty of slit trenches all around we dived for cover.

The air stank and a thin veil of dust arose all round like the wood being covered in a morning mist. I was in a trench with Goodrum and Ounsley and a shell hit a tree just to one side. I thought it was the end. When a short break came we peeped over the top and were horrified to see a tank about, say, half a mile away at the end of the wood. Then we heard the gunners giving fire orders over 'open sights', i.e. angle of sight zero. The tank burst into flames. Awful sight. Tanks rarely operate singly and the gunners went on shooting but we had to get our heads down again as another stonk started. Had a nip of whisky from my flask all round and Ounsley who looked awful asked me if I had my New Testament with me and would I read something to him. Goodrum told him not to be so bloody morbid as if this was our last moment and Ounsley assured him that he thought it was – any second.

When a lull followed I shouted a roll call – we were all in trenches a few yards apart – and it seemed a miracle everyone answered. The gunners had ceased firing and we got out. I went on ahead through the wood to find some information from the gunners. They had some casualties. Found a Lt who advised us to stay under cover until dark as there were still tanks about. He confirmed the previous intelligence that the 12 mile stretch of the valley had to be cleared and told me how to get to Sedjenane. It seemed an eternity since we had seen the place. Returned to the chaps and opened up our emergency chocolate rations. Awful stuff but will put us on a bit.

Shortly after 8 p.m. we moved off out of the wood and within an hour reached the outskirts of Sedjenane. The first thing we saw was that the hospital building with a big red and white cross painted on the roof had been badly hit. There must have been awful casualties inside. By 9.30 p.m. had found the unit HQ and Major Porter the 2 i/c who much to my relief complimented me on getting out. He said he expected to see us the previous day and was not giving us much longer before he would assume the worst. There was no mention of Lt Davies' 'do or die' message to stay put.

Had some food and a wash. I could sleep standing up. Sent for to an 'O' group. Situation east of the town explained. The left flank attack had succeeded and the Germans had succeeded in reinforcing to some strength in the open stretch outside the town. We had to keep Sedjenane at all costs. I was to go to Sgt Jack Bland along a road in open country where his gun was in position near a mound by a bend in the road. Plenty of trenches so we got our heads down. Smoke shells landed in a dead straight line to our front and everything seemed so confused we had no idea who was supposed to come round the bend. The smoke was either part of the pulling out process or for a counter attack. We did not know. Much artillery had been lost and we had been told Bofors 40mm would have to be used for any possible ground target. Jack moved out of the trench and crawled to the gun, traversed it slightly to aim at zero to the base of the mound. He then sent Jack Cowlam to the mound to report what he could see if anything. We watched him crawl back in some haste only to say that on the edge of the smoke, on a track, was an armoured car, moving slowly. Jack moved immediately to the gun. He insisted on being alone. It was already loaded with armour piercing shells.

He made a slight adjustment to the traversing base and then a smallish armoured car slowly came in to sight round the edge of the mound. I saw Jack reach up and alter one of the traversing handles and stood up fully to look through the sight. Then with his hand and in a crouching position pressed the firing pedal with the gun set at automatic rather than single shot.

I could not believe my eyes. Whether the first shot was a hit I do not know but there was a puff of black smoke and then three Germans climbed out, hands above their heads but moved away from us round the mound. At that moment Jack followed by Jack Cowlam hurried to the mound and chased the Germans into the scrub. We heard tommy gun firing and then an almighty explosion as the armoured car literally exploded and ammunition flying everywhere. This alas caught Jack Cowlam right across his chest and he died in Jack's arms almost in seconds. The three Germans were killed but Jack said he would never know if this was the result of the exploding ammunition or whether he killed them. He did not hang about to find out.

Sgt Bland became the first in the unit to be decorated winning the M.M. and Major Porter the M.C. We were told that the blocking of the road way by the armoured car had provided valuable time to save the last of some infantry to get out. We then had to move out and took up a position on the east side of Sedjenane. We were told that the D.L.Is were about to put in a counter attack and that if it failed we would have to go to support them.

We lay and watched the smoke screen – just like the text book. A slight breeze helped to cover the whole line. My heart sank when I saw through my glasses the glint of steel which meant that bayonets were fixed. The smoke stopped, there was heavy machine gun fire, small mortars and then all was quiet. The Germans had extended themselves and had been halted.

3rd March 1943: addressed by the C.O. today and he said Sedjenane would rank as our finest hour even though in some respects it was regarded as our baptism. He said we had experienced some of the bitterest shelling in the whole campaign so far.

4th March 1943: went on the back of Tom's bike to Beja for a replacement Bofors. Found an army bakery and had our first bread since leaving home. Marvellous. Got back at 3 a.m. The chaps slept in the QL which went with us but I was glad to keep Tom company on the bike. It was a beautiful night, crisp and cold. We sang all the way back, glad to be away from Sedjenane.

5th March 1943: moved early morning to Djebel Abiod Cross Roads. Plenty of shooting but never hit anything. Told today the position is serious. If the Germans capture Djebel Abiod they would be clear to Beja where all our supplies came from and then there is only the one straight road back to Algiers. All the first Army must be in Tunisia now.

[Undated:] Spoke to a Sgt in the Welsh Guards who said their orders were to hold Abiod at all costs until there was time to plan a counter attack. Had some good shooting but not good enough. Our Stifkey Stick is marked for 400 mph but the Focke Wulfes do more than that. There were some JU 88s but they were too high. Our range is only 1000 yards. The FWs wanted another 50 notch on the stick so the layers had to almost guess. Not bad shooting though, more minus than plus.

9th March 1943: took up position in a silent role in a narrow valley to guard some medium artillery in preparation for counter attack to take Sedjenane. Made an awful boob getting there. My map reading is usually good but we overshot the mark in the dark and found ourselves right on the edge of some German positions. If the track had been any narrower we could not have man-handled the gun round or if the Bosche had been a little more alert he would have had the lot of us. I found later I was not the only one to make this mistake. We were not too late in position. This is a silent operation – no firing or movement in the day. A Heinkel came over to have a look just before last light but we were well camouflaged.

18th March 1943: had to go to an 'O' group. C.O. told us the Germans were mining the only road between Djebel Abiod and Sejenane and the way they were doing it was to come out from Bizerte in small boats to get right inland and then through a

66

copse or two and scrub land to the road. I had to take ten men and guard an area of road where there was special access from the sea. Moved in position at last light. Felt a bit uncomfortable but if they were only small boats they could only be three or four to a boat and there were eleven of us with the advantage of cover. We sat back to back by trees with double guards. This was a trying business as you had to keep absolutely alert the whole time.

19th March 1943: Bob Goodrum called me early as he had been on duty with Casey in the night. Trouble always follows Casey. He dozed off in a sitting position and Bob said he actually snored for a time. Said nothing for the time but re-arranged the duty roster to put myself on with Casey. He did not twig why. Shortly after midnight he dropped off. We were sitting on empty petrol tins and I eased myself off his arched shaped back to go and fetch Goodrum. Kings Regs and all that demanded a witness. All very unpleasant. The chaps could have murdered poor old Casey. I charged him, put him under close arrest which we could ill afford to do for numbers and sent him back at first light with a message to Major Porter. He was then put under open arrest and I had to give evidence etc. This was done in the back of a truck. Casey went away for a Court Martial and most probably the maximum field punishment. No-one seemed to regret his going. He was cleaning the gun flare once and when he had finished he put in a fresh cartridge which you are not supposed to do and fired it just missing Wilmot. Another inch or two and Wilmot would have lost a knee cap.

20th March 1943: third day on guard but not a sign. Road has been swept clear again.

22nd March 1943: return to the silent valley and counter attack barrage started at 3 a.m. Medium artillery – so we expected a visit at first light to find them. Sure enough, 3 FWs came and we had a go. No hits. They went off. They obviously saw what they were looking for because some Heinkels came later in the morning and bombed the valley – quite heavy. Not a sign of our own aircraft. The range was luckily right for us and we had a go. I have officially claimed one hit on one Heinkel. Fin and rudder hit and thick black smoke coming out of body of the plane as it turned away. We did not see it come down in our sight but if it got back, it would not fly again for some time. Cheered the chaps up a bit as God knows how many rounds we have fired for little reward. Lt Mann smashed up in a motor cycle accident today.

23rd March 1943: moved to Tabarka today for two days' rest, clean up etc. Issued with some new kind of de-lousing powder. Sprinkled it on all our clothes. Had first bath for five weeks in an icy cold stream. Grand. Wrote home. Borrill found half a dozen grenades today and said whilst he was washing in the stream he saw some fair sized fish. We went out towards last light to see if we could catch any fish with a couple of grenades. The noise would not alarm anyone in the Bty lines as we would be well away. All that happened was we killed a score of fish and they all sailed merrily on down stream and we could not get at them quickly enough because of the distance to run between taking cover and the grenade landing in the water. If we had aimed the grenades nearer the bank we might have had a fish supper.

25th March 1943: Djebel Abiod recaptured and it looks a devil of a mess. Met some Ghoums who are to take part in the final thrust for Sejenane. These are French Moroccan troops. Dirty, sly looking and ill-disciplined. Rumour has it that the Bosche runs like mad if he knows Ghoums are about because they fight with knives and are paid so much per 'piece' of a human they bring back. One Ghoum showed me his little bag tied to a cord under his long cloak and there were finger ends, ear lobes and so on. In the final attack on Sejenane the Leicesters were told to stop at a certain point and they did so, but the Ghoums kept going and spoiled everything. The Germans as a result though, fell back further than expected. Rest came up quickly to start sweeping.

26th March 1943: Sejenane recaptured. Almost all of it now in ruins. I have never seen such destruction. Sent to deploy round 71st Field Regt as they had been attracting some attention. Worst air raid was mid-morning shortly after in position. Some incendiaries used on the wood to drive the wagon lines out on to track and then the Germans sent a final three or six aircraft a minute or so later when you thought the raid was over, to attack the vehicles. We fell for this only once. Night bombing is unusual so far but there was quite a heavy raid tonight. Flares were dropped first and we all felt the planes were so low that we should have a go. This we did, fondly trying to shoot down the flare.

All had a ticking off for this raid. It was a trick and since we all fired tracer, the enemy pilot had just to watch a rough circle of tracer to pin point a possible vulnerable point in the centre and he would not be far wrong. This he did and dropped his bombs all round the Artillery and their wagon lines.

27th March 1943: had sharp engagement with 3 FWs at first light. All over in a matter of minutes. Shooting much better and more confident. One brought down but we did not hit it. Off the slot of the Stifkey Stick which meant they were at more than 450 mph. Our range limit is 1000 yards – not easy. Borrill did another good job with the Bren as one came at the back of us. The old trick of one each way. No one hurt.

6th April 1943: pulled out of action and assembled further back as a Bty. Rumours of big move to another sector.

Detailed for burial party. Had to happen some time. Allocated Jeep, gear and had to see Sgt Major. He told me to take two or three bottles to leave Regt number in. Told where one body was but did not recall where the second was. It seems the war is over but only for 6 hours. Both sides to bury their dead. There were four of us. The evening was cool and clear. Found the first without difficulty. He lay a few yards from the track, one arm to his side, partly decomposed. No signs of a wound but around him were smallish shell or mortar holes. We looked around at what would have been his last sight on earth. We were in the valley between Sejenane and the Ridge and "Greenhill" and "Baldy" so for us the place held special significance.

The earth was soft, a reddish brown with lots of small stones to start with but the going got harder as we progressed. We miscalculated the length a bit and I shall never forget the moment when two of us were about to pick up our shovels again to put on an extra foot when Ounsley just gave him a push to make him fit. It would have been hard to alter the length with the body in place.

When the earth was replaced, we made a small cross out of some twigs and put it at the head of the grave with the bottle inverted with his number inside. There was no weapon to be seen. We then had a little service. The Lord's Prayer followed by a reading. I had no idea what to choose so I read something from Revelations about a New Heaven and a New Earth where all was light. There followed half a minute silence and we moved off.

Could not find the second one. Reported to Bty Sgt Major and handed in the identity disc and he asked me to confirm we did not use a blanket for burial and that boots had been removed. I said this had been done. Some time ago we were ordered that some graves, our own and German, had been mutilated by natives to obtain blankets and boots. The Germans as a result booby-trapped their graves and as a result we never went near them. We did not booby-trap ours.

10th April 1943: news came of a move to Central Sector Northern Front and the whole of 139 Brigade or what seems left of it has to come under the Paratroop Brigade for now until it is reformed.

14th April 1943: took three whole days to move. Through Tabarka, Ain Draham, Fermana, Souhk-el-Chemis, Souhk-el-Aba, Le Krib, El Aroussa to Central Sector. On arrival at hide-out, saw the Welsh Guards coming out of the line. What a sight. Obviously about all in, but heads high, not a word spoken.

15th April 1943: moved to another hide-out near Medjes-el-Bab. Birthday amongst the cactus plants. Some three feet tall.

[*Undated*:] Moved to front facing Goubelat Plain for the last lap to Tunis. Spirits were high but after the hills we did not care much for the open plain. We were deployed to protect the 6th Armoured Division. What a stirring sight as they came along the dust road. They fanned out after they passed us. They stopped a few hundred yards in front and some crews got out for a final check. We doubled the stand-to in this period and then suddenly they all mounted, moved forward to below the brow of a hillock and then charged over the top.

Not long after they disappeared we moved to protect the Welsh Guards Brigade HQ and then heard the start of the tank battle. We then had to form two huge rings of AA round the tanks which were following on the first lot and we were in the outer ring. A hectic time was had by all. On two occasions we had to fire from the pads without them down, i.e. on the wheels as there was not time to prepare. We had practised these crash actions but never had to do any until now. We were very quick and the barrage from the full circle was unbelievable. No aircraft penetrated to the tanks. Our own air support arrived only just in time and with events moving swiftly on the plain we were withdrawn to Medjes-el-Bab to protect some more armour moving up.

23rd April 1943: God for England, Harry and St. George. Lovely morning. Moved to wadi to protect 71st Field Regt. This unit had 25 pounders and seemed to have a lot of calls for targets so we knew our stay was not going to be peaceful.

24th April 1943: had a trying time this morning. MEs and FWs for breakfast and long periods of 'stand tos' in blazing heat and queer insects. Water short. At noon we were heavily bombed by our own Mitchells. We stood to and identified the planes then as about to stand down, saw the first stick of bombs drop to our rear. We dived for the slit trenches in case the next stick caught us and then a remarkable thing happened. One of the escorting Spitfires left his station and dived down in front of the leading bombers and no more bombs were dropped. Intelligence Officer told us today that only one obstacle was in the way before the final break through to Tunis and this was an enormous feature known as "Cleopatra's Tits". It is said the Commandos and some Guards are moving up to take these hills.

25th April 1943: moved today to Pont du Fahs, near Bouarada to cover a wide open position from which real armour had been taken and dummy tanks and guns made of cardboard put in their place. We had to turn mobile and dart from position to position as part of the bluff. Only had one engagement today – a Junkers 88. He took photographs we think but he hid in the clouds after some good shooting but we did not hit him. We had a lot of "plus" shots very close and he dropped all his load on the next detachment on the move.

27th April 1943: taken out to rest in a wadi, clean up and get stores etc. for final lap. We were told one final attack could probably bring about the fall of Tunis and early evening several hundred bombers came over to plaster the edge of the plain before Tunis and the Cap Bon Peninsula. We could see in the distance the opening barrage of the 8th Army which had started from Alamein the previous October and were now at the outskirts of the other side of Tunis. This put us all in great heart.

[*Undated*:] Moved forward over the plain behind some armour to St. Valeri. Had a hectic time and nearly running out of ammunition. We were far too close to other vehicles and some armour – we must have been a first class target but the few visitors we had before our own aircraft appeared did not penetrate the circle. A lot of petrol has been lost to the Germans in the sea crossing to Bizerte and Tunis which probably accounts for their lack of aircraft.

7th May 1943: forward troops entered Tunis but no cease-fire sounded. All bombing had stopped because so many prisoners had packed in to the Cap Bon area hoping to get away, plus our own troops chasing them.

13th May 1943: cease-fire sounded in Africa. We ended up on the Oued Zarga–Medjes-el-Bab road and watched thousands of prisoners coming in. Total lot said to be about 240,000. Some walked, some rode. One German asked Ounsley for a drink and Ounsley called him a Bastard Hun and refused. There was nearly a scene until an MP sorted things out. Told to keep in action in case of any isolated raids from Italy but none came today. In the afternoon I was sent for to sort out a few awkward prisoners who had detached themselves from the marching columns. There was no fear of any of them running away – there was nowhere to run to now but the problem was obviously going to be water, food and enough barbed wire. Many of the wells had been poisoned anyway and all our water came by vehicle and was rationed. These Germans wanted to borrow razors to shave and refused to get back so a Cpl and I took off all their braces, made them line up and they all joined the never ending column, not at all pleased. They were much older than we were and went to some pains to tell us they were not Nazis and so on. Some were arrogant and said the defeat in Africa was only a set back and they thought the whole of the Med was still theirs. There had been some cruel propaganda somewhere but we bundled them off with the truth.

16th May 1943: officially stood down. Had to help with barbed wire fences for prisoners. Terrific heat. Some of this lot also arrogant types and thought they still held Algiers and Casablanca and that the war in Africa was not over. One said in excellent English "You will not beat us in Europe". A lot of colourful abuse was hurled at this one. So that was that. Our heads were high and proud to be connected with the name of Alexander and the British First Army.

19th May 1943: attended a V day parade in Tunis followed by a day out in this 'Paris' of North Africa. Nothing was organised of course and in general terms we had not much of a time. How could it be otherwise. The place is as smelly as Algiers anyway. Went in some lovely gardens which had not been touched.

20th May 1943: all had to turn out extra smart and highly polished today for a VIP. No-one ever says on these occasions who is coming. We lined a dusty road not far from our tent lines and in a matter of minutes with a breeze blowing were covered with dust and sand. We were immediately in front of a German 88 Tank which had been knocked out and lay at an angle across a ditch. This position turned out to be fortunate because we were the only ones who overheard a conversation between Mr. Eden and Mr. Churchill when they arrived. There was a lot of top brass around but we heard Mr. Churchill say "Anthony, come let us look inside" and Mr. Eden was up in a flash quite sprightly and an aide gave Mr. Churchill a lift up when Mr. Eden grabbed his arm. It was all over in a minute or so. Mr. Churchill looked old and ill. He had a white suit on, big white hat, the inevitable cigar and made the V sign as he moved off to rousing cheers. Mr. Harold Macmillan Minister of State in the Middle East was also in the party.

21st May 1943: moved to Hamman Lif. Very attractive small sea-side resort. Had a really good time on the first day. Heat was terrific and we spent most of the time in the sea or lying at its edge watching masses of B 19s going over to bomb in the direction of Pantellaria.

22nd May 1943: sent out today on a salvage drive having to report the position of burnt out vehicles, tanks, recovering ammunition, etc. In the sea again this evening. To look at the Bou Kornine, about 9,000 ft in the twilight is something I shall remember for a long time. The sea was luke warm. Have never known such peace and quite for a long time. Very odd – I was in the sea with the rowdiest lot you can imagine and we all lay still and looked up to the mountain. It was one of those occasions to remember and to know that each other remembers too as if it was something very special. So it was – all we could hear was what seemed like a thousand frogs croaking in a scrub area of the beach.

24th May 1943: a day to remember where the Gods were kind. We sleep in the open with mosquito nets tied to anything upright and always follow a tight drill last thing at night for both making up the area to sleep on and tucking in the net. I woke up to find a black scorpion half in and half out of my right hand side trouser pocket. We sleep fully clothed minus boots. What woke me up and made me look straight to my side I shall never know but I remembered the Doc saying that if ever this kind of thing happened, keep absolutely still. I tried to draw the attention with a half whisper of Cpl next to me but he was hard on. I lay a few moments feeling somewhat frightened. A sting from the black one is fatal fairly quickly and the brown one bad enough if you have hospital attention quickly. My inside seemed to be thumping thirteen to the dozen. To my relief Sgt Vipond came by on his way to the bog. I caught his attention. He stood a bit petrified and ran off like mad. I wondered whether this was to secure help for me or to attend to nature, the needs being accelerated by the sight of his first scorpion. Anyway, he came back with Bob Goodrum both with spades and in a few minutes I had quite an audience when word had got about. The others had pick handles. The commentary which followed was really unbelievable to say that for me it was a serious moment which could end quickly either way. If the scorpion crawled inside my pocket I would have to try to get the trousers off quickly without provoking it to bite and if it went the other way, get out of the net with all speed. Ounsley said "Hey Sarge it's a black 'un". I know that you fool. Vipond gave a description as to how it lay for moving – in or away from the pocket at which Bob Goodrum suggested it could change its mind anyway. All this to whispers of "keep still". It was not very funny. Someone suggested they go for the Doc. The scorpion solved it all. It moved. To my everlasting relief it went down my backside, on to the blanket and towards the edge of the net. I flung myself out of the opposite side and disturbed the net so that the scorpion was thrown off the blanket on to the sand and down came the crashing spades. The dismembered pieces even wiggled in the sand as the pick handles thrust deep in to the soft golden sand. A passer-by who did not know the facts would have thought us all mad. I watched all this only too thankful to be out of it all.

The Doc then appeared and told me I was very lucky indeed. He took the pieces from Vipond for his talks because he only had drawings for his lectures on do's and don'ts in the desert scrub. He said if I had jumped out as soon as I saw it, the ending would have been very different. Despite the cool morning air I was perspiring heavily and the Doc insisted I lay down a while in the sick tent which I did with a smashing cup of tea.

Went to the pictures this evening. Cinema had a sliding roof which remained open until about 5 minutes from start of film. Heat terrific. Some mail from home.

26th May 1943: went sick. Prickly heat. Also 16 times to the bog yesterday. Doc said not to worry at 16 but if any increase could be suspected dysentery. Could scratch myself away – both arms and one shoulder.

27th May 1943: nine times to bog today an improvement. Prickly heat not responding much. Sea water seems to make it feel easier. Heat unbearable and every siesta time spent in sea.

31st May 1943: no more than mild diarrhoea now and prickly heat spots beginning to go. Sleeping with gloves on.

14th June 1943: whole 46th Div. assembled in convoy to move 680 miles to Beaufarik, west of Algiers. Covered 137 miles in first day. Sleeping by side of our vehicles. Double guards. Slower progress today over mountains through Ghardimaou to Souhk Arras.

16th June 1943: deluge of rain in night and we all woke up about 2 a.m. in a violent electrical storm and lying in about an inch of water. Rest of journey through desert and scrub dreary and monotonous. I read a little when the roads were not too bad and shared some of the driving with Ounsley.

23/25th June 1943: Brigade occupied an orange grove. Unbearably hot. Had to turn out to assist the Tanks in an exercise when they did a full scale invasion of the coast at Zaraldo. Visited a farm near our lines and made very welcome with grapes, wine and prunes – far much more than we could eat or drink.

28/29th June 1943: had a weekend in Algiers and saw Betty Grable film at the ABC. "*La veuve joyeuse*". Also went to the opera house. Walked a lot and went to El Biar, a most beautiful spot commanding a magnificent view of Algiers Bay. Ate a lot of fruit. From a view of the bay it was obvious to all of us that something was afoot. Big operation in progress judging from the landing craft and other vessels whereas we thought we might, with everything finished in Africa, be going home.

15th July 1943: from making my last note until today, we have stuck the heat, the humid winds from the Sahara, millions of flies of all types, mosquitoes, butter like water, corned beef like liquid out of the tin plus all the wonders of the African soil. Saw the film "*Mrs. Minniver*" in Algiers where things are better organised now. Our KD in cinema literally soaked through. Have had some spells on aircraft co-operation and air to ground signals with the RAF. Afternoons too hot to stir.

[*Undated*:] Operation "Husky" – the occupation of Sicily – now well in hand. Told today that we were first reserve for "Husky" if all had not gone well. At night we watch the new Lancaster Bombers on the shuttle service between home, bombing Germany or Italy on the way out, land here and repeat the process on the way home. Very hot again.

[*Undated*:] All Sgts reported to Cap Mtifou for revision of aircraft recognition. Did not last long as all recalled to base for move.

8th August 1943: moved to Blida. Terrible mishap to American destroyer in harbour. Blew up with heavy casualties. All the natives ran out of the dock area and never came back. Frightened to be blamed I suppose.

9th August 1943: all split up for land and sea journeys. I went to Hussen Dey by train for a night in a transit camp and boarded a Trooper called *"Ban Fora"* at 1900 hours. Had dinner with Lt Adams. *Ban Fora* was captured at Dakar and had done two trips to Sicily. Still no idea where we were going. Parted with all our gear and large kit.

10th August 1943: only two troopers in convoy but kept close in with a destroyer to port and one to starboard with a corvette leading. Beautiful evening. As we pulled away from Algiers another destroyer came at full speed to the starboard side and as it was pulling in to station I read a morse message from our ship "Why are you late?". I read as the answer "I have been detained" only to be followed by a further signal from our ship "Obvious. Why are you late?" and the reply to this was "Oil pipe defect now in order". The pilot left us after this and the evening was uneventful.

11th August 1943: lovely day. Sea calm and blue. Both destroyers carried out ack-ack practice by firing a target up on a parachute and bringing it down with remarkably few rounds.

13th August 1943: Friday the 13th. Nasty job disembarking in a heavy swell. Drew in to what was left of Bizerte harbour. Wrecks all over the place and convoys coming in from Sicily. Had a long wait because of a shortage of berths and then it was decided to disembark us on to LCIs 300 at a time. It was no mean feat down a rope ladder from the *Ban Fora* and then to jump at the height of the swell on to the deck of the LCI. A sailor demonstrated first while we watched. We managed it with only one injury but a few lost kits as jumps were made. Assembled on a jetty which seemed in a state of collapse and then set off for bivouac area 9km. Marched through centre of

Bizerte which was just about laid flat. Hardly a building had escaped. The few civilians left just stood and stared. Some turned away looking for their belongings and their houses. No-one smiled.

14th August 1943: reported sick with a swelling on the left half of my posterior. M.O. said I had been bitten by a lizard but the orderly promptly reminded him that lizards did not bite as a rule. They had a thorough examination to try and find out what had caused the swelling. Went to open-air cinema on a hillside to see "*Hellzapoppin*". Could not sit down because of my seat so had to stand at the back and could not see very well.

16th August 1943: everything possible being done for our entertainment. Swimming sessions, open-air cinema each evening. Went to a concert given by the crew of HMS *Uganda* and *Lord Roberts*, two Monitors. Lay on the hillside before turning in and read morse message from the leading vessels in returning convoys from Sicily. Mostly in code and the only clear message oddly enough was the number of casualties for which ambulances were requested.

18th August 1943: Germans must know we are making use of the harbour and probably know of the assembly ships with some of the fleet. Not surprised to have an air raid. Quite a heavy one and we lay in holes in the hillside to watch. The search lights were the latest type, guided to the target and it was amazing to see how quickly a plane was caught in the beam. Saw three direct hits in this way. One was a ball of fire and exploded in a few seconds and plunged in to the sea just clear of the harbour. The other two hit the far side of Bizerte.

19th August 1943: more units of Fleet arrive during the night. Heavy smoke screen put over whole harbour before last light in view of another bright moon. Our Corps Cdr hurt in back and one leg in last night's air raid. Splendid to see some of the Fleet today. Defiant, gracefully dotted about the bay.

21st August 1943: managed to get Nat Gonella's autograph on a 5 Fr note at a concert. Lots of swimming, P.T. eating grapes and melons. Sea water nearly healed the sores and marks left from the prickly heat.

22nd August 1943: had to report sick again about my posterior. Swelling worse and area very hot. Doc said poison was ready to come out. Took trousers down and lay face down on trestle table. Two orderlies sat on me to keep me still. The Doc lanced my seat and drew out a green coloured thing like a small match stick. Very painful while it lasted. The lads insisted on rigging up some mirrors so I could look at my seat and see the egg-shaped lump which was left. No-one really solved what had bitten me but the Doc insisted it was a lizard.

26th August 1943: moving tomorrow. Went for last swim for some time. Ate lots of melons. Kit check and pack.

27th August 1943: moved to a concentration area where we were told to rest pending embarkation. No-one knows where at the moment. Pleasant vineyard to stay.

28th August 1943: final test of water-proofing of vehicles. No news.

29th August 1943: could hardly stand the heat so went with Bob Goodrum to floating dock where everyone swimming in the nuddy and came back at end of siesta time. Having nothing to do and not knowing what is up is not very good. Some papers arrived from home and two letters.

30th August 1943: heavy air raid early on and heavy ack-ack. Open-air cinema again. Called to an "O" group and told embarking tomorrow. Destination not stated. All the Brigade is going.

31st August 1943: operation "Husky" over. All Sicily ours.

Embarkation cancelled and back to vineyard.

6th September 1943: embarked on LST *371*, one of the Kaiser wonder ships built in 11 days in America. Found we were only one of a large task force. The lake and harbour full of activity until last light. Everyone amazed at the way ships are moved about and formed up – a master planning somewhere. We began to hope everything else afoot would go as smoothly. After threading our way past scuttled ships and narrow openings we formed up in a line outside the harbour. We are in the centre of the convoy, third down, middle line. A nice feeling. As if waiting impatiently for the convoy to form, there were two fast Cruisers HMS *Aurora* and HMS *Penelope* dashing up and down and then they were joined by destroyers and a big ship the like of which had not been seen before. Rumour has it it is the *Coventry* which is a flak ship firing what they term "Z" batteries.

Read a little before dozing off.

Here I think ended a chapter in the annals of the British 46th Division and the British First Army. Morocco, Tunisia and Algeria plus all the desert to the Middle East were all free at a terrible cost. We had seen the once proud Afrika Korps beaten to the ground. Churchill referred to the Battle of Egypt as being "the end of the beginning" and he said the next task was to tackle the "soft under-belly of the Axis", a task which had been started by the occupation of Sicily.

PART THREE: ITALY

7 September 1943 to 26 February 1944

7th September 1943: heavy air raid last night did not seem to do any damage to convoy. Told to check emergency rations (48 hrs) and ordinary rations (48 hrs). Our LST crammed to capacity and after watching food, ammunition, medical supplies plus the hundred and one items of paraphernalia of war loaded onto our ship and others, we all moved off – a most impressive sight with a large escort. All the talk on the ship was about the Navy and the comfort of the escort ships and not anything about what we are all supposed to be on. The time was 11 a.m. when we watched the rusty coast line of North Africa fade into the distance. No information of any sort had been given to us and all we could gather from the sun was that we were travelling east.

Glorious morning. Most could not help feeling a bit despondent because it was obvious we were going to take some part in a landing somewhere. All the vehicles had been water-proofed. The day was uneventful and we just lay about the deck in the sun, hoping there would be some official information soon.

8th September 1943: another glorious crisp morning and clear sky. Late afternoon we were spotted by what looked like a Heinkel, normally a bomber but also used as reconnaissance and sure enough we had a visit about last light. Unfortunately I was below deck with a few others having a snooze when the alarm went and the metal lid slammed down on the deck. We were closed below. Then heard a lot of ack-ack and knew the raid was on. I think we were less scared the first time in action

82

in North Africa than when we were shut off below deck and we were all relieved when one of the crew opened up. We had missed a spectacle from all accounts as two planes were shot down by some Mustangs which had appeared from somewhere. With long-range tanks they could have come from Sicily.

When night came we felt uneasy about the space on deck as the LST was packed with men and equipment and a long row of ammunition boxes down the middle. There seemed hardly a spot on the deck to lie down which was not within a yard or so of ammunition boxes, so much so that there was nothing for it but to adopt a careless attitude about it all. There was nothing we could do except to go below which we did not care to do. It would all go like one big bomb if we were hit and on that happy note we had a last cigarette before the order came to darken ship. It was at this point that I read in morse a plain language message from the ship in front that Italy had capitulated and had signed an armistice retrospective to 3rd September. The message ended "Press Association, Reuter and Special." Within minutes the news was given off by the Captain of the ship. Twilight comes quickly in the Mediterranean but there was sufficient light for an Intelligence Officer to call all Officers and Sgts to the bow of the ship when it was revealed we were heading for Salerno and that our estimated time of landing if all went well was H plus 16. H hour was to be 3 a.m. in the morning of the 9th.

9th September 1943: first light was called to the bow again and shown a chalk map of the boot of Italy, drawn on the metal deck with a more detailed plan of Salerno and surrounding country. Emphasis was placed on a rail track about 1½ miles inland which had to be reached within a matter of hours of landing. The Hampshires of 138 Bde 46th British Div. were to follow the Commando and recce groups and we were to follow the Hampshires.

Turned out to be a glorious morning and we saw the Apennines coming down to the sea in precipitous cliffs. Amazed to see on looking round the bay the extent of the shipping plus what seemed to be the best part of the Mediterranean Fleet dashing up and down. We all felt there was far too much shipping in the bay and something must have gone wrong somewhere.

We lay in between HMS *Lord Roberts* and HMS *Uganda*, two monitors with 11 inch guns and we could see the gunners stripped to the waist in the morning sun, belting shells off like fury. In the middle of this came the worst air raid of the passage to Salerno Bay. The flak ship HMS *Coventry* lay the other side of us and she opened up with everything. There was hell let loose for quite a spell. We lay on the deck face down. Only one bomb came near LST *371*. The raid then moved over to the other side of the bay and we saw one FW 190 brought down with thick smoke coming from it.

An announcement was then made to all ranks. It was a warning that the landing would not be a push-over just because Italy was now out of the war. Intelligence reports had reached the convoy since our part of it left North Africa that opposition was to be expected from the Germans.

We lounged about all day on deck and everyone seemed to be getting a bit on edge. We knew the Hampshires had gone yet the Navy were still bombarding the beach. We saw the bomb flashes. Towards last light the monitors started again and we noticed the angle of sight of their guns was zero. We began to feel sorry for the chaps somewhere who were giving them their targets. Early evening we moved up the column but could not see anything apart from a few gun flashes from well inland. Dozed a while and at about 11 p.m. there were sounds of a fair number of aircraft which we knew by the sound were German. Probably Junkers or Heinkels. HMS *Coventry* again sent up salvo after salvo and the din was terrific. AA guns from destroyers opened up and then flares were dropped. Seemed more powerful ones than we had ever seen before and the whole bay seemed as if it was in daylight. Only a few bombs screeched down near us and the body of the raid seemed to be on the supply columns spread out the length of the bay. We did not seem to have any night fighters about as the AA guns went on all through the raid. Very relieved when it was all over. Dozed to first light.

10th September 1943: saw for the first time Green Beach. Shells seemed to be landing on it from all sides. The Navy were shelling the edge and the Germans also firing on it from the mountains behind. At noon, news came that all was not well. 128 Bde and the Hampshires had failed to reach their objectives. Worse was to come. The 56th Div was said to be in difficulties and part of the USA 5th Army could not land on their beach, further south from Green Beach because apart from heavy opposition rumour was the beach was not suitable. This seemed to us an awful blunder but the IO said it was a fact. There had been no time to test it apparently in the week between the fall of Sicily and the new landing at Salerno.

This was not exactly morale-boosting news. We stood and watched Green Beach with some anxiety. The whole time-table was out of gear now as we ought to have landed behind the Hampshires but only the commando and recce units had got ashore. What we took to be German 88s inland fired out into the Bay. We could see nothing hit but the whole area was full of sitting targets. Then a couple of destroyers came charging down almost to a few hundred yards of the beach edge and pounded away at some target. The 88s stopped. Sheets of flame shot up inland coupled with a few dull thuds so we presumed an ammo dump may have been hit but those destroyers certainly cheered us a lot. We saw no movement on the beach and no-one knew what had happened to the troops who had got onto the beach. We could only guess they were lying low somewhere until the Navy finished off the big guns behind. We had no artillery anywhere near landing.

About 3 p.m. a lone FW 190 came nosing round. Every conceivable gun opened up and down it came in a ball of smoke, crashing into the sea. No-one baled out. The sickening sight of the crashing plane ought, I suppose, to have made us pause a while to realise the futility of it all but the news was so bad, and we did not want another air raid, that the mood was tempered accordingly and the chaps actually cheered when the plane hit the sea.

Evening drew on and we were overdue to go at H plus 16 now.

Nothing happened. Night time seemed the obvious period to get on the beach but we lounged about with little sleep. Watched the flashes of the big naval guns far out in the bay and still the *Uganda* and *Lord Roberts* banged away. Just before last light we saw the hospital ship *St. David* come right to the edge of our column to take off casualties. Despite the large red crosses on the vessel it was shelled by heavy stuff from the mountain. A destroyer raced down and laid a neat smoke screen round it like some anxious bitch looking after a young puppy and then we saw *St. David* pull away through the smoke and away to North Africa with her first load. We were told we would probably go in at 9 p.m., to check our gear and be prepared for battle. Usual string of orders. Then it happened. The alarm went and AA guns started from the Navy almost at the same time as we realised there was a large number of aircraft upstairs. A stick of flares came right over us and it was like daylight. Ammo boxes were stacked all the length of our craft and there was nothing to do but lie down and hope for the best. One had a very inadequate feeling as there was just nothing anyone could do. Bits of AA splinters were landing here and there on the deck. Then came the awful screech, louder and louder of a stick of bombs. Seemed like an eternity. Then came a crunch and the whole ship lurched when a huge wave rose higher than the ship and came over us. The ship steadied again. The flak ship kept firing all the time and as the drone of engines faded away we got up and saw a blazing ship in our line about half a mile away. We were glad we had moved forward a few hours earlier. Ten minutes later this whole process was repeated but with no near miss this time and we were unscathed. The Naval beach master must have signalled to land immediately after the raid because no sooner was the second finished than the signal came to beach. The engines on the LST revved up with a mighty roar we had not heard for nearly 24 hours and we charged for the beach letting the anchor down about 100 yards from the edge in order to winch itself off.

At this time the naval bombardment started again and we were relieved to find their targets inland and not on the beach. We were aware of the crunch of the shells a fair distance in front.

The jaws of the boat opened and after hours of training in water to waist deep we simply stepped off the ramp into not more than a foot and without a word spoken we filed fairly quickly to aim for two shaded signals to indicate the safe lane leading across the flat beach to some sandy dunes where we had been told to assemble before moving off.

As I lay in the grass growing out of the dunes I had a quick roll call to find all present and was about to set off to find Capt Davies to report when I noticed a dark figure, motionless a few yards away. I felt a slight tingling sensation when I recognised a German helmet on the body. Hoping he was dead I moved across to make sure. He was quite dead. His war was finished. I was tempted to go through his pockets or pinch his watch but there was not time. I was told later that the manner of this chap's death was vital intelligence. He had been drowned. This proved the bosche had had a rehearsal for a landing on this very beach perhaps only hours before we arrived.

In ten minutes from landing, we moved off quietly following tapes through a large vineyard and met some Hampshires and Commando, their faces all black. Their news was grim. They confirmed what we had been told on the boat that the initial advance had not gone well and that there had been a lot of Hampshire casualties. As we moved along a path, a message was sent to me that I had to halt at a large house at the end of the vineyard and wait for orders. On arrival we spread ourselves out to the few strategic points and quietly waited. There then started the most terrific stonk – worse than we had ever had in Africa. The house was hit several times and it seemed yet another miracle that we were all unscathed. A Major of the Hampshires arrived and asked who we were. He said the position was serious and that we had to be prepared to fight for our lives before first light. We had to stay where we were. He said we ought to have been astride the Naples–Salerno main road the other side of the railway track but that we had not reached the track yet. He had lost the greater part of his Company.

The Navy bombardment seemed endless and there was pandemonium on the area of the beach we had left. Machine gun fire was very close now and we were deployed in the end of the yard near the edge of a copse. My orders were to allow nothing down the lane to the edge of the copse which led to the yard and to shoot at anything which moved in the arc immediately to our front.

Everything was pitch black and I'm sure we saw things move which were not there at all. There was no question of giving away our position as everyone who had got to the beach was in about a mile radius of it and the Bosche knew that.

Borrill let off a few bursts into the edge of the copse and we all followed suit but it was an occasion for split seconds to count because what bothered me was if anyone made it to the edge of the copse – not difficult in complete darkness – we would be done for if a few stick bombs or hand grenades landed on the concrete yard. Because of this we got over a stone wall and took up positions between this and the edge of the copse on softer ground. Heavy machine gun firing was further round to the centre of the beach head. I would not want to experience this waiting, not knowing much of what was really going on coupled with utter confusion, ever again. Then to our horror a couple of figures loomed out of the darkness right in front of us. Neither had a helmet on and it was difficult to tell friend from foe in the conditions when someone shouted "hold it – they're Hampshires". I ran across a few yards only to find no Hampshires at all, but a couple of Bosches, arms round each other's shoulders, both clutching a bottle in their spare hand. Absolutely tight they were. We relieved them of their weapons, took off their braces, and sent a chap down to the beach with them. They could hardly stand and must have each consumed the best part of a bottle of horrible smelling stuff like red wine. They would be in their thirties perhaps. I often wondered if these might have been the first prisoners at Salerno but probably not. What happened to them I could not imagine as there was no room for us and our gear still to come let alone cater for prisoners. They only failed to be shot on leaving the copse by a shout from the yard to "hold it".

We had no artillery ashore yet but luckily a recce carrier was sent to our position and Lt Brown appeared to take us to another assembly point. Things became quiet about midnight and we were told to try and get an hour's nap before first light when a German counter attack would be obvious.

Full stand to at first light. Our position was on a slope in view of the beach. Materials and men had never ceased to pour in all night and there did not seem much beach as such left. It would have been a gift for aircraft but none came. Everyone wanted to hear our own 25 pounders but none fired. The expected counter attack was held by 128 Bde and the Germans fell back a little but gave it out to the world the landing had failed and the British were evacuating the beaches.

Our role as temporary infantrymen was over and we were told to collect our Bofors which was on another LST. The beach was so packed it took some time to find who was who and then report for the first deployment. This was to take up a position at the end of the dock area and join in the AA barrage as artillery and heavier units were expected to land at the docks later in the day. Having de-waterproofed the vehicle and checked everything I sent the Bdr ahead as coverer. He returned considerably shaken with shelling and some sniping on the main road to the docks. He said he thought we only had half the town and doubted if anything would survive very long in the dock area. This was in full view of the mountains where there were obviously observation points. The shelling was accurate. Anyway, we set off, pleased on the one hand to have something positive to do but feeling a bit grim nevertheless.

Lt. Brown called in a hurry. Said the Germans had re-taken their end of Salerno and if I could not get onto the end of the dock road along the front I was to find a suitable site as near as possible to it. I told him the coverer had said in his opinion nothing could survive on the dock road but he said we had to try.

Lt. Brown recommended we load with armour piercing shells before moving off in case of any German armoured cars or recce units about, which reached the dock road. It was at this point we heard our own 25 pounders for the first time. Very heartening. Their targets seemed to be over the dock area and beyond – so long as they did not shoot up the dock road. Lt. Brown said he would go forward for a recce and we pulled off the road behind some bushes to wait. We then saw a woman of about 35 come staggering towards us from the open space between ourselves and the start of the dock road. She was dazed to put it mildly and spoke modest French. She had a small child and between us we pieced together that her husband was 'missing' and two of her children had been killed by a shell. She said the Germans were in the end of the town and asked where to go. *'Dove andare?'* That was about all we understood of her Italian. To turn back was out of the question even if she made it to the German area; to go forward towards the beach was also not without many hazards. I gave her a tin of bully and a packet of biscuits and sent her off. She seemed too grief-stricken for tears. She also said *'casa finito'* – house finished – so I presume she had no home and maybe lived in the town.

Lt. Brown returned somewhat shaken. News not so good. He said he thought we could reach the end of the harbour road and the best time to try this would be last light but not to go beyond the first block of buildings. The Navy and our 25 pounders were still banging away. Our only hope was that the Germans would lay off the harbour road on the grounds that it ran into their end of the town. With little light left we moved off and waited at the end of the dock road to try and pick a spot. The only cover was the buildings facing the water-front and I decided to put the gun, leaving it on its wheels for a quick departure immediately opposite a large building like a warehouse, even though this might restrict the arc of fire if any aircraft came in the morning. The position also commanded a straight patch of the dock road for any vehicles moving.

Any position seemed an alarming one to stay for any time. Left a guard on duty and we all went into the battered building. The time was ripe, I thought, to plan a quick move if we had to and what to do if attacked along the dock road. I was between Borrill and Goodrum when a shell landed in the water about 50 yards from the break-water dead in line with the gun. Lt. Brown had been right to say not to move until dark. I presumed we had been spotted as about a dozen more shells arrived, all spread between about 100 yards in the harbour to the road opposite the house. One landed on the tarmac road and caught the front of the building but none of the chaps were hurt. We simply lay down beside the gun and hoped for the best. The run across the road was not worth it to the building. After a lull we dashed across and lay behind a pile of rubble in the entrance. I think the Navy had put a few big ones in this building. Another barrage then started and lasted for about ten minutes. The very earth seemed to quiver. These were mortars and those which landed on the harbour road had a much longer lethal area. Few landed in the sea to either side of where we lay. Both sides then seemed to have had enough for quiet followed and at about midnight we tried to get some sleep. There was so much hanging debris and what not in the building, we moved outside and stretched along with the rest of the rubble, by the pavement side with legs tucked well into the wall. I think we slept for not more than four hours and the guards were changed hourly because it was too much of a strain for longer periods.

It would be shortly after four o'clock when the whole of the harbour road received the most terrific pounding. To say it was a dark night it was excellent shooting but they had had a few hours of daylight to get the exact range. We had no option but to dart into the house. We lay down at the extremity walls and I did not know I was under a precarious piece of hanging plaster and brick work and then it happened. The top of the building caught one and down it came. I was covered in cement plaster and dust but there were no injuries apart from a few bruises. This stonk lasted for some time and caused two injuries at HQ and one vehicle out of action. A large shell splinter went through the roof of our tractor, splitting the framework and other pieces hit kit and lockers. The petrol tank and ammo escaped.

Dawn came to Salerno with an indescribable beauty. The mist half way up the mountains, a clear sky and to the left, towards Green Beach, a pall of smoke still lay over the town itself. No news of the battle had reached us now for 24 hours. All we knew was that we had been shunted to the harbour road because of landing supplies operations and the Germans must have known or guessed this because of their attention to the harbour and road the previous day. We all felt very weary, were unshaven and also hungry. I hoped for some orders from somewhere as I could not see how we could survive in our present spot. We were obviously under observation. On the other hand, there was no prospect of an air raid on the harbour with nothing there to hit.

A D.R. then arrived and said we had to move to a landing strip in the course of preparation, near the beach. The news was not good. The beach head was not considered firmly established yet, the beach itself was still crammed, no armour had landed. With air support too far away in the Sicily air fields some Spitfires were to accelerate their arrival and we had to protect the RAF Field Regt who were constructing the air strip. Before we moved off we saw a huge smoke screen put down by the Navy to shield the beach from OPs and then through the screen a small naval vessel went like mad to the jetty. Just what this was about we had no idea but it was under a constant hail of fire from the other side of the harbour. The skipper certainly had some nerve and luck for he got away alright. We were about to move off when Lt. Brown came and said we had to stay where we were because it was believed some AFVs had infiltrated in the night to our end of the town and could make for the harbour road. We re-loaded with armour-piercing shells and put ourselves at the junction of the main side road to the harbour to wait. Nothing happened for a couple of hours so we moved off to find the landing strip.

The pall of smoke still hung over Salerno and as we came near to the beach were amazed to see how packed it was. The unloading parties must have worked like heroes throughout the night. Although this does not seem to be tank country we heard there was a full armoured Division at sea which could not land yet. Possibly this was why we were sent to protect the harbour with good access roads. Anyway, ours not to reason why etc.

We obviously had to sink the gun in a pit and on arrival at what we were told was called Sugar Beach landing strip, I met an RAF Regt Officer and scrounged from him a bulldozer for not more than half an hour. The soil was light and the driver did a grand job. We had a useful pit in no time at all with the gun in it and ready. We were told Spitfires were expected at first light.

Dusk came, the mosquitoes bit fiercely, a brew of char, some emergency rations and a little sleep. Machine gun fire and some artillery seemed a good mile or more away but there was always present the feeling that a strong counter attack could put us all back on the beach, if there was room. The Hampshires we heard had paid a heavy price to reach the rail crossing.

At about 9 p.m., planes were heard, no flares were dropped for some time and no-one fired a shot. Our Bofors has a range of only 1000 yards and this is when you can see the target. The planes went away. Half an hour later they brought their friends and pandemonium reigned all around the beach head. There was no heavy ack-ack landed as yet. Cliffe Raine and I lay behind the earth pile for the pit as there was not time to get to the slit trenches. His detachment was about 75 yards away. Suddenly without the usual screech a bomb dropped very near and either a splinter or part of a butterfly bomb caught Cliffe high up in one leg. His vehicle was put out of commission and one other was wounded. I did not know at this stage where medical help was. By nothing short of a miracle none of my chaps were injured though our vehicle was well and truly riddled again with the tank spared.

I then got Cliffe underneath my vehicle. He drank two full bottles of precious water. I put a first aid bandage dressing on him, stuffed some cigs down his jacket and wondered how I was going to get him out of it. In the books I used to read about the first World War there would be a shout of "stretcher bearer". Not now. Robinson 99 then appeared, crawling across an open space almost in daylight with the flare, and asking for help. His Sgt had disappeared somewhere and not returned, one wounded and vehicle out of action. I told him his Sgt was under my truck wounded. Robinson was after the same as I was – a first aid chap or the whereabouts of a First Aid post. I left Cliffe and set off with Robinson to try and find the RAF Reg. first aid man. I did not know whether to chance it across the open strip or crawl round the perimeter. Bombs were dropping all round the area and the flares never seemed to cease. As one went out another two seemed to replace it. We had to have a breather half way round and Robinson then told me he had been hit in the neck and back. Robinson 99 was not one to complain. He had crawled right across the strip in that condition. I had a look at him and he had a hole in the nape of his neck about the size of half a crown. I put his field dressing on that and was about to get his trousers down to look at his back when I thought it was the end of the world.

We were in a bit of scrub which gave no protection at all and we ought not really to have stopped but there were two near misses either side of us and then a mass of small explosions all around us and a few feet from the ground. These were the new type antipersonnel butterfly bombs which are released from the main canister at a certain height and then fly to the ground with little wings. We did not know this at the time. We pressed on in a few minutes' lull and mercifully found a medic. He put Robinson in the RAF Regt. first aid spot and then went back with me to see Cliffe. He was rather white but quite calm. All he could say was that when I had a minute would I write to Mary. The wound was inspected for signs of gangrene and then a loose door appeared from somewhere on which Cliffe made his departure to the Beach and hopefully the hospital ship *St. David* which we had seen two days before. What a mad business this all is.

We had had severe shelling in North Africa but no air bombing like this. We all felt a bit scared. Apart from some spasmodic shelling the rest of the night was quiet. We did two hour guards and the rest dozed.

[*Undated*:] No entry has been made for a few days but we are now told that up to ten days we have not been out of danger in making a re-embarkation. There have been few nights without air raids but the strip was only once attacked in daylight. Our accurate fire drove them away and their bombs all fell wide. We did not hit anything. Only one Spit was damaged by any raids but eight were damaged when they arrived from Sicily because the strip was too short. When this was spotted a chap stood at the end of the strip and for every plane where its wheels did not touch down at a certain spot he shot a red Very light and it revved up to take off again.

As late as 27 and 28 September, nearly three weeks after the landing, unloading transports were still under shellfire on the beaches. Day and night a ceaseless toil continued. The armour landed on the beaches during darkness and it was a comfort to hear tanks rolling off the transports. At this period the Germans mauled 138th and 139th Brigades and launched a huge counter-attack in an attempt to split the beachhead in two. He very nearly succeeded.

On the morning of the 28th we were in a sort of copse with an avenue down the middle, and some armour was hidden on either side of us. At first light we stood to and three FW190s appeared with little warning right out of the sun. They machine-gunned straight down the avenue. The Bofors had a limited arc of fire, but all hell was let loose for what was a matter of a minute or so. Then a tragic thing occurred. Mallinson, the CO's batman, a faithful and stout fellow if ever there was one, grabbed a Bren and began firing from the hip at the FWs. Unfortunately he pressed the trigger before he had raised the Bren enough and caught the CO on the backside. The CO was evacuated immediately and Captain Davies took over as acting CO. After the counter-attack failed, word got round that we were safe, and the Germans began to withdraw.

On the 29th we moved to Ponte Cignano rather disturbed by rumours that our infantry had had 75 per cent casualties and that our role was to be changed.

30th September 1943: moved forward to Cava. V.P. to protect what seemed to be left of the town.

4th October 1943: moved forward to Nocera. The V.P. we had been given could not be reached until some enemy rear-guard had been disposed of. Under heavy rain we slept on the pavement for three nights. Some very queer spots have started all over my face and neck and the mosquito cream stings badly but is a must at last light. Must see the Doc if they don't go.

5th October 1943: the enemy we are told is in full but orderly retreat. Reported 'O' group at last light.

6th October 1943: moved forward through Pompei and Naples out on to the plain of Villa Literno. Naples was an absolute shambles and chaos everywhere. Hundreds of people asking for food, no bread or light and infected water supply. Main post office blown up. Site at Villa Literno a bad one. No V.P. given to us and told to wait as likely to move up to the river Volturno tomorrow. Shells dropped all around us at intervals all day. The 25 pounders were in front and the 55s behind. Very heavy rain. This horrible feeling here again of not knowing when the next shell is coming. Why the devil we have to stay in this exposed spot I can't imagine since we have not been given even the 25 pounders as a V.P.

8th October 1943: vehicle and gun stuck when getting out due to heavy rains. Had to winch the gun out first and then winch Bedford out with anchor on firm ground. What a job. Late for assembly to move to forward area just south of river Volturno. V.P. given as assembly area for Bn of Foresters who were to cross the river. We are under observation here to make matters worse and had more shelling than few days ago.

The Foresters ran in to point blank fire at the other side of the river and were repulsed. Jerry followed through and re-crossed it again. We were not aware of this and had orders to move up behind the Foresters for ground targets. The old man came up just in time to pull us out.

We have stayed in this spot for twelve days and feel we have had more than enough of this constant shelling. Some FWs and ME 109s came over a few days ago but we did not hit any. Tonight I was chatting at last light outside the bivvy when there was an almighty swish and thump. We did not hear the usual whistle and flung ourselves to the ground. After a few seconds' wait we crawled to some trenches and waited a while. By then it was quite dark and we were mystified at what had happened. No-one seemed to have a clue until it was suggested the thump was a dud shell. At first light we were amazed to see that it was – well and truly buried with a mass of earth around it and dead in line with where we were standing at the time. Not more than 50 yards in it.

19th October 1943: big attack is on to cross the river and we have to move forward to give directional fire with tracers. Not very nice.

20th October 1943: complete change of orders for Brigade. Moved further inland to Francolise. The run there revealed hopeless chaos and destruction. Roads were bad in the main and Capua was literally razed to the ground. The move was done at a fast and furious pace. When we did stop we had to dig trenches, wait and then move on in stages. Francolise had been a hot spot but now was not attracting a great deal of shelling but what there was, was bad enough. Our Vulnerable Point (V.P.) was to protect some Field units, 25 pounders forward of Francolise. Whilst waiting to move forward, we were put in a copse with Bde HQ 22nd Armoured Brigade, the old desert rats. They were in fact to take over our positions when we had gone.

It was a clear day, sunny although cool and whilst we were hanging about waiting for orders, a couple of Gerry prisoners came in. The Intelligence Sgt of Bde HQ set out a trestle table in front of a tracked vehicle and we saw a Capt. appear, sit down at the table with a map and in came prisoner no. 1. He looked about 40, smallish, dishevelled and generally a surly type. He walked to the table. My German vocabulary is lacking somewhat but I did understand the Capt shout at him to "stand back". He made the prisoner stand some yards from the table. The conversation was too fast for me to follow much but I did get some of the answers and they were not very co-operative.

The Capt. was obviously not making the progress he wanted

to with this chap and he called the Sgt who took off the tracked vehicle a pick axe helve, clipped on the side. He walked to the prisoner and stood behind him. Once again some questions were fired at him and he refused to answer. The Sgt just grabbed him by the scruff of the neck, bent him over and gave him six of the best across his bottom and upper limbs. More questions were fired at him and this time the Gerry answered but I could not get much of it. A lull in the proceedings then followed and I spoke to the Intelligence Sgt who asked us to move away. The Capt did not like an audience at these interrogations. The prisoner was then taken away and I saw him lolling against a vehicle with a guard having been given a mug of tea and a cigarette. Prisoner no. 2 then came on the scene and to show willing we moved away a little but kept in a position to see everything. We knew little of the Geneva Convention but did not know this beating of prisoners went on.

The Sgt had told me this Capt spoke fluent English, French and German, was Dutch by birth and had escaped from Holland in 1940. He had had terrible experiences, having seen his own wife raped, his children taken away from him and so on. There was a deep hatred in his heart for all Germans. During the desert campaign it was said that he adopted brutal methods to get information when intelligence was short and he would start his interrogations by telling the prisoner of his past experiences in Holland, about his wife and children etc., so they knew at the start he really hated them and meant business.

Whether Prisoner no. 2 had heard the beating or not I do not know but he was more forthcoming and gave much more than his "number, rank and name" which is all one is obliged to do. Within ten minutes he was sitting beside the Capt at the trestle table pointing out things on his map and having a cigarette. Later the Sgt told us he had pinpointed two large ammunition dumps, given details of battle casualties, malaria casualties, identity of his unit and much more.

We saw them bundled in a P.U. and were gone. Their war was finished.

26th October 1943: the Gustav Line defences had been reached now and the going was slow. Sent forward to V.P. The gunners seemed to be in an exposed position and we were on a slope to their side also exposed. We dug the gun in, camouflaged the bivvies and settled down.

27th October 1943: stand-to at first light. Lovely crisp morning and good visibility. The gunners had an early target and were firing ranging shots before we brewed the tea. We then had the comfort of six Spits patrolling but not for long. Quiet morning. It was here we had our first proof of German atrocities. We had heard tales of course but could not credit some of them. It reminded me of the old days in the Scouts when you sat in a circle and a message was whispered round until the last one had to say what it was and as a rule it was very different from the original whisper. Things get exaggerated. From the side of a hedgerow to our right two oldish women came running shouting "*Inglese, Inglese, bambino, bambino*" and the rest we could not understand from our very modest vocabulary in Italian. By gesticulations it became clear that "Tedesco Officers" (Germans) had ordered the fingers cut off some children – their children presumably – because they would not talk and give information. Both the women broke down and wept so we did what we could to help them although this was not much. I managed by saying "*dove*" (where) to get the name of the village from which they had come and how far away it was and also their names. We gave them a tin of bully beef and some biscuits and sent them further back. I then sent a runner to HQ with the brief information I had.

9th November 1943: moved forward of the gunners to a VP which was an important bridge and still intact. It was vital this remained so because contact with the enemy had been lost following a breach of the Gustav Line in front so it was essential reinforcements could use the bridge. Luckily I was not the V.P. gun which was actually yards from the bridge. It was here we suffered our worst casualties for at about noon, coming out of the sun, 12 FW 190s surprised us as we only had seconds to stand-to when hearing planes and then it happened. They literally fell out of the sky in line and whilst all hell was let loose at them, the V.P. gun caught a direct hit and killed all the detachment including Sgt Oxberry, excluding only two who were seriously injured. They only came round the once and we scattered them all which probably resulted in the bridge remaining intact. The Col. played pop that with such a set piece we did not bring about 50 per cent down. Arthur Turner's gun had a rough time. Two chaps hit in the neck and one who looks like losing a leg.

11th November 1943: leaving site took many hours due to thick mud and heavy rains. Had to winch ourselves out. Returned to concentration area for a rest and maintenance. I was lucky to come out of the hat for four days' rest at the divisional rest camp in Salerno.

Our four days very pleasant. Salerno was starting to "live" again although there were many food queues. Rubble was still being cleared from the streets and there were signs civilians were returning to their small farms. We managed to get to the ancient ruins at Pompei and saw the amphitheatre, market place, wealthy Greek houses with mosaic floors. Some had vomiting rooms. It is said it was an insult to one's host if you did not retire after a meal to vomit. To do so you went to another room with a small well arrangement in the middle.

26th November 1943: on return from rest, we were deployed along Auto Strada 7. With gradual air superiority we only had rare visits from Mes and FWs.

12th December 1943: moved forward into Gustav defences. Heavy shelling at Concha and Vezarro Nr Rochamonfino. We carried on through this and no-one hit. We moved then into snow-covered mountains in hard conditions. Digging holes and getting in them seemed the only way of keeping warm. Life has few comforts if any. When we could sleep at night we covered ourselves with straw found from old barn type shacks and often in the mornings there would be a thin line of blood along the finger joints even sleeping with mittens on. Shaved in what was left of our tea. Water not reaching us so frequently and when it does arrive it is heavily chlorinated.

14th December 1943: a perilous journey through the mountains towards the plain and river Garigliano and the entrance to the Liri Valley. We were so high that despite the heat of the engine oil pressure dropped and the going was bad even with chains fitted. During the last part of the journey the road was narrow and we failed to negotiate a bend properly with the result that the gun slipped over the road edge and on to a bank, nearly taking the Bedford with it. We were well and truly stuck. All the convoy stopped behind us but not for long. A major on a motor cycle turned up within minutes and played merry pop with us saying we were holding up a full Brigade and ammunition etc. He therefore instructed me to disconnect the gun and let it slide down the bank and proceed without it. Easier said than done but with a bit of brute force we managed to separate it from the tow bar and two tons of Bofors slid a good 20 yards away from the road. The column then moved which pleased the Major and he disappeared looking foul.

At a convoy stop later the Major appeared again and told me, in a bit better mood this time, that the spot where my gun lay on the bend was under observation during daylight and it would be a tricky job to retrieve it. Pleasant news as I knew who would be sent to pull it out but I doubted if our winch rope would reach the gun anyway. By now we were in full view of Monastery Hill and Monte Cassino. Through the gap which it guarded lay Cassino itself, one of the reputed strongholds and almost impregnable ones in Europe. Cassino in the distance was being heavily shelled and we saw the end of a terrific barrage going down on Monastery Hill. No-one doubted that the Abbey was being used as an observation point.

We were not given any V.P. but when gathered together I regretfully reported the temporary loss of my gun. No fuss at all. Just hard luck but I had to go back the next morning with REME to extract it. The uneasiness returned of operating under observation the whole time but we managed to get away with it and REME did a grand job in an hour as we were held up with other traffic moving up on the narrow road.

15th December 1943: return gun to Baty workshops for inspection and repair.

17th December 1943: moved to Concha in a queer position by a way-side shrine which we used as a cook-house. No sleep. Bitterly cold.

18th December 1943: dug lower into ground so as to fit together two 25 pounder empties to have a fire. Very cold and some snow. Great preparations in all quarters for Christmas with extra Naafi rations, beer, tinned turkey and a bottle of whisky. Had a good mail from home.

25th December 1943: O.C. visited us today. Had a good dinner by Pte Moody ACC. A good time was had by all but the war goes on. Sang some carols at night.

28th December 1943: moved to protect some 55s who were at zero feet and we are stuck up a fair hill. Moved into an old cottage where an old man and his family had just returned from the caves. He is a weird character and we can't quite weigh him up. What we don't like is the fact that each night he disappears for a long time and there is really nowhere to go forward. It would be a long and hazardous walk to the nearest village in the rear. I decided to ask him "*dove andare* etc." and he had the nerve to say he was a member of the resistance and had been out doing the work of a saboteur. There was never a smile or a twinkle in his eye – you could not tell whether he was telling the truth or not. He said he knew where all the Gerry positions were and he knew all the area like the back of his hand. He offered to take two of us with him next time, but there never was a next time.

After we had questioned him he never went out probably thinking we might follow him, who knows.

31st December 1943: had a message to return to THQ and leave the gun for stripping moving then to a rear area to wait. Here we dug in and repeated our fire building with some cartridge cases. I slept feet to feet with Bdr Goodrum and we felt sure the fire was out when we dozed off. Alas not so and luckily we both woke at the same time to dense fumes and a scorching roof of the bivvies put together as one tent. We were both fully clothed except for boots and we had no option but to get out as fast as we could and sound the alarm. This happened at 2 a.m. and the guard was at the other end of the track. He heard us shout, he too shouted for the other guard who picked up the first can he saw and came running to the scene. It is a firm rule that all water cans have a white strip on the top because otherwise they look like jerry cans of petrol. The one which was poured on the tent was petrol, not water and the whole thing went like a bomb. We had left our small packs, top coat and boots. It was impossible to recover anything. I was up before the old man the following morning to explain the whole affair and there was a hell of a row about picking up the wrong jerry can. I got a ticking off for having a fire and all in all it was a heavy price to pay in the end for the sake of some spam and one egg which we managed after a very long time to consume when we had the fire going. Trouble was we did not have the flue right and the breeze must have changed.

1st January 1944: a New Year's Day in the Apennines [Vezarra, near Monte Cassino]. The night was bitterly cold and Heaven's fleecy clouds passed in and out amongst the light of many stars. Alone, they hung, to shine their twinkling light, yet whilst alone together in one great union, looked mockingly at Earth. They showed no sympathy for our lot, no longing to be here, just heavenly bodies, apart, giving out their noble duty, precious light. The "seven sisters" hung together hand in hand and twinkled each in turn. They have their peace, so far from Earth and constant in their nightly shine they seemed to say "We wish you peace this New Year's Day. We know you watched us full of wonder, from grey Atlantic to Gibraltar, from blue soft seas to stormy straits. Through all these months we've given you light, so you can see the dangers of the night. But this is all we do. Nor is our wish to come to Earth, but shine its way to better paths of peace and calm once more."

So spoke the stars as they hung so bright. The clouds defying their light for seconds raced on to block more light. In the dark, beyond our peak there lies a monster Monte Cassino. The lonely sentinel looked up. How bitterly cold it was. The wind seemed to pierce the very blood and freeze him to the ground. He moved his legs, They were stuck in the hardened mud. He pulled them out and moved slowly across the grassy slope. A fierce wind came in gusts, the clouds raced by to block more light.

Four hours of the New Year were gone in part slumber until the duty called. The sentinel let his mind wander. 'Resolutions. What happened to the last ones? How long will new ones last this time?'

How long has he been abroad? More than a year. How time passes. What a year it has been. A hard slog, death, destruction and misery with no end in sight. But there was a victory. The fact we are where we are is a victory of sorts.

'Hush. A noise. Stand still, keep by the bush. Move now and you may not move again.'

"Halt, who goes there?"

"Friend."

"Password?"

"Bramble."

Response: "Bush."

Safety catch off.

"Advance, friend, and be recognised."

"Pass friend. All's well."

Silently, the sentinel wandered up and down the slope, listening, looking, wondering. Suddenly like a warning shell shot burst a wind of gale force fury lashed the bushes and trees bared now of all their summer glory. Lonely, thin bare bodies battered unrelentingly by a merciless wind singing an eerie mysterious whine of protest that puny trees should bar its progress. The sentinel turned his back. Too painful now to face the mighty gale conscious of the fact that all too soon a storm of such ferocity as yet unknown to him would unleash itself.

Was all in order at the point? Would anything be blown away? Had he been wise in the setting up? Too late now to make and mend. Something buried in the snow? As he turned the darkness denied the sisters of their light and through the wooded slopes far below and at his side, on swept the rushing violent wind likened only to the noise of a giant waterfall.

The lonely sentinel looked around. All was dark with no pretty falling flakes dropping slowly to earth to warn. There came upon him a mighty fall of snow each flake as if in frenzy to reach the earth. In half an hour it wiped away the many paths and tracks and slowly crept up the tree trunks painting the earth the purest virgin white. Then mocked the storm as did the stars!

"I am the mighty storm," it said. "No man can harm me, no puny human stop my rage. I cease when earth is covered white, no mountain missed, all valleys swept. I hide the light of mighty stars. I conquer all, the King of Storms. I come and go throughout all time as I have done of yore but you live to fight and die so soon."

With hysteric whine the storm tore at the ridge with unabating fury.

The sentinel saw the light of dawn, though late and soon he found no mountains, trees and peaks of world renown, no valleys, roads or long lost sheep but all was wrapped in thick grey cloud. Hidden too the evil Monte Cassino.

So comes another New Year's Day to lead us on to hopes and deeds, to bring the sentinel to one place where the mighty storm could not molest.

Hope springs eternal in the human breast they say. Let us hope a way forward and out of these wretched mountains may soon be found.

4th January 1944: recovered gun and moved to tunnel site. In front of Cassino. Saw 75 Fortress bombers unload on Cassino and after this many hundred more in box formation, what is called "blanket bombing". Saw little of any enemy planes. The flat valley in front of Monte Cassino across the river Garigliano is one of the worst spots to imagine. Everything and everyone seems to be under observation and Gerry must be able to know well in advance of all movements. His heavy artillery reached us today. Most unpleasant. We all seem to be very tired and jumpy with this shelling although we have not been really forward for some weeks.

[*Undated notes 1944*:] Major preparations for the battle for Cassino and then the break out into the Liri Valley. Most depressing to see these huge mountains and to know Gerry is at the top of them in the Monastery and seeing everything.

Noise of reinforcements, ammo convoys, a few tanks, goes on night after night.

Moved to forward area to protect 788th Fd Regt 25 pounders. Lucky we are not the mobile troop which has gone further forward to give directional fire for the infantry.

13th January 1944: the 25 pounders must be doing well with their targets because they attract a fair amount of shelling. Improved our pits today as there seems no pattern to the German shelling which is all over the place.

14th January 1944: had a visit first light from 3 FW 190s. Spotted them in good time and all hell let loose at them. None hit. Probably come to spot the 25 pounders. As suddenly as the ack-ack started it seemed to stop when 6 Mark 5 Spits came on the scene and we watched the dog fight which did not last very long. One FW shot down and we saw the pilot bale out, the other two got away.

20th January 1944: moved further up the plain. Camouflage heavy. Next Fd Regt 25 pounders. After sorting ourselves out and pits dug, a stonk started such as we have not had for some days. It was reminiscent of North Africa. Heavy rains, bitterly cold and that awful feeling which comes from knowing you are under observation. The gunners are a grand lot. They fired all through the stonk whilst we were very glad to be in the pits.

16th February 1944: stupendous news. The whole Division to pull out and our Brigade to be first. Few hours notice to come out of action and report to a V.P. at the top of Concha Hill to guard the main auto strada. After A and C Troops had passed we had to follow on to Teano. Lt. Gen McCreery came to address us and said we were leaving Italy and that he hoped to welcome us back again astride the river Po at a later date. He thanked us for all we had done since Salerno but made no reference to the size of the Division now compared with last September. It is said we have had 110% officer casualties.

19th February 1944: no idea where we are going except that it is to Naples.

20th February 1944: arrived Africola transit camp. Whole move marvellously organised and quick. All gear and weapons left behind.

21st February 1944: boarded HMT *Sobieski* at Naples. Polish trooper captured earlier in the war.

22nd February 1944: set sail. The view of Naples, Capri, the snow-covered Apennines was very wonderful. I hope never to return to this country again and to the squalor and disease of the Southern part anyway. Journey very comfortable and we had our best treatment yet on a trooper. Through the straits of Messina by the coast of Sicily we took a left turn not right, so we knew at once we were not going home. Destroyer escort and a Hudson aircraft and a calm sea. Mosquitos from North Africa took over later on. A Division afloat is a valuable target.

23rd February 1944: woke up to quite a hubbub on deck as the sun had risen on the "wrong" side of the ship which definitely confirmed we were going what was to us the wrong way down the Med and not therefore going to Blighty. No-one knows where we are going. The crew will not say anything. After breakfast, lounged about on deck and watched the escorts. These destroyers are a comforting sight.

So ends another phase of our travels. Six hard months gruelling at times in the mountains under desperate conditions for spells. The bitter cold and torrential rains are now things of the past and whilst we all seem to have some sympathy for those left behind at Casino, deep down, we all hope never to see the area again.

Wherever we are going, it is surely bound to be for a rest.

24th February 1944: modest breeze and a bit choppy. All ranks had to do P.T. Called to meeting of Officers and Senior NCOs to be told we were bound for Egypt for a rest, refit and reinforcements. Beyond that was not known. Whole of 46th Division to be together, or what was left of it at the present time. Wrote a few letters.

Speculation all around as to whether or not we will not do any sight seeing by being dumped in some out-of-the-way camp or whether we shall be near Cairo. One thing is certain and that is we are sure to be under canvas. One big change will be to have no black-out drill every day.

25th February 1944: this convoy does not seem to go very fast and has to suit the lowest speed I suppose. A member of the crew told me we add a few knots on when it is dark.

26th February 1944: clicked for Ship's Orderly Sgt and must have walked miles today. One benefit is that you have to go round with the Orderly Officer of the day at meal times so that you can eat in peace afterwards. The worst thing is having to report the blackout as it has to be 100 per cent when reporting or there is trouble. Usually one ship signals to another one if there is anything wrong.

PART FOUR: THE MIDDLE EAST

27 February 1944 to 28 June 1944

27th February 1944: arrived Port Said at the mouth of the Suez Canal. The AA gunners stripped to the waist even in February were on the breakwater and envied by some for their "billet". The scene was vivid in colour. Bright green trees, yellow palm trees, pink and white houses and signs of more modern devices than we had seen for some time. A roar went up at the sight of the smalls hanging on the lines from the Wrennery. There were no Wrens in sight. Our escort had by now left us with their usual hooting and we pulled in to a big dock where there was more than enough to keep us occupied in watching for a long time. No orders for disembarking yet.

28th February 1944: disembarked and walked straight to a troop train waiting for us. All cattle trucks. 30 men plus full kit to one truck. Having chased away a number of Arabs and clutching our weapons like gold, we waited etc. It was late afternoon or early evening before we moved off and we made the best of things with intermittent sleep with arms and legs all over the place. I sat at the door for some fresh air and watched the stars appear and in the dim light saw the scrub areas and some fields of crops pass by. There seems to be a semi-black out, neither here nor there. The train jolted the whole time. An awful journey. Managed some sleep and had to stay on train till early morning.

1st March 1944: de-trained and after another long wait a convoy of trucks appeared to take us to Quassassin Nr Tel-el-Kebir. We had travelled West of Cairo. Treat to do 50 mph on a tarmac road and shortly after dawn we saw the camp. It was all made up of ordinary tents on hard earth covered with gravel and interspersed with large areas of sand. YMCA opened specially for us for a brew of tea and then managed some breakfast. So ended a reasonably smooth and efficient move of the remnants of the 46th Div.

[*Undated*:] For the last 14 days we have spent organizing ourselves, sleeping a lot, P.T. and a few ABCA lectures (Army Bureau of Current Affairs). This camp must stretch for miles. Visits to WOs and Sgts' mess were frequent. Long walk but worth it. Also open air cinemas.

In the mess we made friends with Osman Soliman who taught us to count to ten in Egyptian. The waiters are all Sudanese and fine chaps. They would do anything for us. The rest room, restaurant and bar were all marvellously furnished and the place was really like a palace. We had to adjust from Italian liras to piastres. Spent a lot, drank a lot and slept as much as we could. Bob Smith and I went to Kebir garrison to see a good performance by an RAF band. There was a mixed audience of Czechs, Poles, our ATS, South Africans and New Zealanders plus British Nurses etc. Also managed to see the edge of the Western Desert towards Alamein – all very flat but a good road through it. A sand storm came one day – a terrifying experience. Sand gets in your ears, eyes, nose, in bed and in your food. Fortunately it did not last more than a couple of hours and at its height one could not see many yards for fast whirling columns of sand.

12th March 1944: surprise, surprise. The whole Brigade is to go to Cairo for 4 days' leave but in two batches. I am in the second batch going tomorrow.

13th March 1944: lined up for orders to the effect that whilst it was every man for himself in Cairo, if there was any breach of discipline, or trouble with the Military Police, the leave would be stopped and the whole unit returned. Also we had to familiarise ourselves on arrival with the "no go" areas. Went by road straight to "Hotel Manchester". Very comfortable.

[*Undated:*] Saw the Sphinx and the pyramids. There was a queue to get on a camel and we managed it in the end. The one I got snorted a lot and kept putting its green tongue out. The native minder had a job to get it on its feet and he kept muttering all the way about the charge for the ride. We seemed to go a long way for a few piastres. Saw King Farouk's Palace and the sights generally. All very strange, seeing fast cars, crowds jostling about, gay lights. Beer was 10 piastres, about two shillings a bottle.

Night life was hectic. We set off at the WOs and Sgts' club from where we picked up a carriage. The driver said he would not let five of us get in but we persuaded him and though cramped, trotted off to the "Pam Pam" club. What a drive. Hardly anyone seemed sober and the smell was atrocious. We managed a drink of some awful wine after some difficulty but there was nowhere to sit, we certainly didn't like the look of the unattached females as well so we cleared off. As we moved to the main exit through the thin string beads which covered it, a couple of naval ratings were being turfed out and there was a scene. Knowing we had to keep out of any trouble, we moved on. Found another buggy and this time went to the Moroccan Club. Just as we were trying to make the cabby understand where we wanted to go, a Lt in our Brigade, don't know who he was, trotted up on a good looking steed. He had apparently borrowed it for the night. The "Moroccan" was more select and we found an empty table when five quite pleasant hostesses came across and in good English asked us what we wanted to drink and could they sit with us etc. They waited on us and we were well and truly taken for a ride. As the rounds went along Sgt Tommy Mochan, a dour Scot and with a temper, picked up one of the girls' glasses when she wasn't looking and took a whiff. It was odourless so he took a sip and said it was water. We had been paying for gins. We ought to have known the gins were showing no effect anyway. Old

Mochan hit the roof and got up to go to the bar. We saw trouble coming. Two of the girls disappeared. Then in a flash three of the heavy squad (locals) moved across and asked us to leave. We said we had done nothing and saw no reason why we should leave. One of these three then returned to the bar and another of the heavy squad appeared which made four against five. By this time Mochan was shouting the odds and I wondered if they understood his broad accent. Other tables were now watching and a chap came across to ask what was the matter. At this, the remaining girls left and the heavy squad stood together a few feet from our table just glaring and presumably awaiting the outcome at the bar. At the back of our minds was the fact that the leave was not over and we did not want any trouble.

We agreed it was better to leave and got up to go to the bar and try and persuade Mochan, having said his piece to come away. The heavy squad followed us so we were all at the bar now. No one swindled Tommy Mochan though, and got away with it and the minute one of the heavy squad took hold of his arm he swung round and landed him one. At that precise moment, which took us by surprise, I felt a powerful pair of arms grab me from the rear, under my armpits and we were all sort of frog marched like that out of the place with Mochan shouting he would bring the police and all sorts of colourful references to the club, its staff and so on. I'm not sure they knew what a thieving bastard was but this came out a lot but it was all over fairly quickly and we were on the main steps with the heavies lined up to make sure we did not turn about and go in again. It would have been all up with us if any CMPs had been about, yet we were quite innocent as to the cause.

Went to a cinema show and before the film started the roof opened and we sat looking at the stars. It was very hot for March. It was an English film. At 10 p.m. we had a discussion as to exactly where we were since we all had a clear understanding of the map in the hotel entrance which all ranks had to understand. We thought we were about the middle of the area in which we could move freely and stopped a cabby to ask him to take us to another club. He misunderstood us or else acted deliberately, and dropped us in an out-of-bounds area. The first thing we knew about this was when we saw the usual sign and made him stop immediately. We paid him, having failed to make him understand and go back. He insisted he was taking us to where we asked and it all became a bit heated. There we were in the brothel area. No sooner had he moved off, than we were aware there were no troops or for that matter many people about. We were in short lost as no one had paid much attention to all the turns in the cab until we saw the "no go" sign. Fortunately, we were all sober. The area was dimly lit and we set off to try and find the name of a street to see if it might ring a bell with the hotel map but no luck. There was a maze of small streets and turnings. A small boy ran towards us and in perfect English offered us the services of his two sisters for 200 piastres. My sisters very pretty, good time and so on. Now we knew without a doubt we would be in trouble if spotted because the CMPs had a habit of combing the no go areas. We could not get any sense out of the lad as to where we were or how to get back to the bright lights and when he knew he had no customers he ran off the way he had come.

We tried to think how long we were in the cabby and to estimate his speed. We could be faced with being a mile or so wrong and what disturbed us most was that we could not even see the bright lights or glow of a big city in the distance. Whether or not this boy knew the police were about we shall never know but not long after he disappeared, we saw far in the distance what we knew to be the headlights of a jeep. No mistake. We turned and ran like the wind taking the first turn we came to, hoping it was not a cul-de-sac and waited. The vehicle approached along the main street slowly and sure enough it was a CMP jeep. We had not been spotted. The clatter we made running was bad enough so we let a minute pass to allow the jeep to get further up the street and then we started at a trot what was in the end to be quite a run. Fate was kind to us as we had no idea in which direction to go but we came on a street with better lighting but alas still the out of bounds sign displayed on the wall. We then recognized where we had been dropped by the cabby and went in the reverse direction. Our troubles were not over. Feeling it would be better to keep on the wider streets rather than the many small side ones, we must have gone a mile when we stopped in our tracks at the sight of two CMPs standing with their backs to us, but well in the distance underneath a street light. Their attention must have been elsewhere but they never moved, whilst we literally tip-toed back and took another turning. We saw their red caps clearly. We then heard the noise of traffic which we had not heard for some time and ran towards it. If there was traffic there would be people and we could mingle with the crowd – anything was better than this dark mass of small badly lit streets. We quickened our pace and came to a huge wall which went up a slope and so far as we could see in the poor light seemed to curve round the whole area we had been in.

We reached it just at the right spot for there was a hole in it just about big enough for a body to get through. We pushed another stone or two out and crawled through, feeling somehow we were safe. There on the wall was another no go sign and this time we were on the right side of it although in an awkward situation if caught there. The other side of the wall had a scrub bank and we scrambled down it to find ourselves nearer civilisation. We felt very thankful for the hole in the wall. We could so easily have missed it.

17th March 1944: last day. Very hot. Wandered down to city centre. Had another unfortunate incident this time with a shoe shine boy. Many had their permanent spots by the curb side but some of the younger ones would follow you asking for "Shoe-shine Johnny" and it was annoying. Sgt Mochan in quite good humour just cuffed the lad – he did not hurt him – and jokingly told him to hop it but the lad was offended and he opened his tin and with his brush flicked some of his polish across our feet and gaiters. Tommy Mochan then did hit him and the lad ran off to tell his big brothers and once again we were in a chase. This time, short, fast and saved by the cinema. About six of them left where they were sitting at the curbside and ran after us down the main street. We had a good start and soon lost them and whilst not setting off to go to a cinema, thought it might not be a bad idea to be off the streets for a couple of hours and we all got in without problems, fortunately another English speaking film. Returned early evening by train to Quassassin.

18th March 1944: Brigade convoy set off for Palestine. Told this was a mission of internal security following a mutiny of some units of the Greek Fleet nearby. Drew all new gear in minimum time a Mark 1 gun with a new tractor. "O" Group meeting. Told Bofors was for "show" as a ground weapon. Trip was really marvellous. Through vast spaces of Sinai Desert. We made good time crossing the Suez to our first halt and then to staging area No. 1. We slept the night in, and on and under our vehicle. Setting off early the next morning brought a few smallish hills but in the main miles of monotonous desert frequented here and there by small Arab tents and "wild men" of the desert.

On the third day we developed petrol trouble. When George had put it right Lt Brown came back to find us and told us to get a move on. The convoy was by now miles in front and George managed over 60 mph out of the Bedford and we widened the gap between ourselves and the Lt who could only manage 55 mph on his cycle. He was not pleased. We rolled up last in a heavy shower. The evening run was unbelievably beautiful and I have never seen so much cultivated land of fruit and vines, all rotting because there were no ships to export it.

Arrived Camp 21 Nathanya, Palestine. Pleasant site. Under canvas on a sandy/greenish patch, we rested and played gun drills each morning. Having made friends with a native guard on a local vineyard, we fiddled some huge grapefruits which we have for breakfast. I was Acting QMS here so had frequent trips out in the jeep which I could more or less call my own.

Trips to Nathanya were memorable. All the way was through orange groves and vineyards. The "sweet scented air" in this land of milk and honey is no poetic fancy.

19th March 1944: day out in Tel Aviv. This means "Hill of Spring" and the general beauty of the city was very impressive. It stands out as new being only 30 years old, against the dirty level of Jaffa. The place proves the enterprise and genius of the Jew. Many educated Arabs live and work there but the main population is Jewish.

27th March 1944: called out to act in an internal security role. It seems the Greek Navy when ordered to put out to sea with some British ships to chase a "U" boat, refused to sail. Crew mutinied and a serious revolt started. This had its effect on land and there was trouble at a Greek internment camp near us. We had to deploy round the camp just for show but not shoot at anything or anybody. Trouble was over in a few days.

8th April 1944: rest of Regt caught up with us and we all moved off to Hadera. The camp was well placed just 400 yards from the sea and in view of the terrific heat even in April, there was a welcome repose in the sea for as long as we liked each afternoon. Compulsory siesta for two hours from noon. The days start at 5 a.m. and it is impossible to do much after 2 p.m. anyway. Mosquito nets necessary in day time siestas. We are as black as Arabs. Time passes quickly with fun and games in the cool of each evening. Saw the Palestine Symphony Orchestra (45 pieces) in Hadera. Quite good.

15th April 1944: 25 today. Party of us went by road to Haifa. Looks much better at a distance with the hills in the hinterland than when you actually get inside it. Not worth a mention. The heat grows more intense each day and gun drills and parades are now held before breakfast. A cloud in the sky is an event of note. K.D. has to be washed on alternate days. Sea salt water has finally cleared up my spots and scars on legs, arms and neck.

7th May 1944: moved to Nahariya, South of Beirut for exercises with new reinforcements, both for Bofors and some ground field work. Very hot. Bofors shooting came first and the Bty shot down seven sleeves. We got one. The whole Regiments broke a camp record with fourteen sleeves in four days. Just my luck when our turn came there was some top brass standing watching us. Shots were all over the place to start with. All minus, then a few plus and the sleeve was out of range. Old man played pop. Next time round we got one.

10th May 1944: field work in the cool of the evenings. Don't think much of some of the reinforcements. They are only 20 and 21 years of age but then so were we when the war started. They don't seem to have had the same type of intensive training as we had. Probably we had more with staying in England long after our training was finished. Yesterday evening went out with Bob Smith to a local cafe. Met a very lovely Austrian Jewess, a refugee from the Nazis escaping early 1938. We sat and talked in the garden and again tonight and she spoke of the Vienna she knew, of her work and home. She did not know where the rest of her family was and wondered if she would ever see them again.

12th May 1944: very hot. Went to cafe again with Bob Smith. Free drinks this time.

14th May 1944: all Bty returned to Hadera. Done to a turn by the merciless sun. Butter is like water and tinned corned beef like butter. You could drink the corned beef.

15th May 1944: O.C. addressed all ranks and said he wanted every man to visit the Holy City as this was a chance not to be missed. Padre would take parties. With few exceptions we are all going to Jerusalem in a day or so.

17th May 1944: the journey to Jerusalem was very beautiful. A beauty of a different kind not seen before. The wayside is rugged and the meadows and fields often full of dark grey and brown rocks and the colours seemed to vary in some way each separate mile. It was amazing. We went to Bethlehem first after a tea and wad in Jerusalem. The pictures one sees of Bethlehem, of people in long white cloaks, white flat roofed houses, the oxen in the fields are all correct. There was a feeling of history and romance about the place. Went to the Church of the Nativity first where the door is shaped like a needle head and saw the place where Christ was born. This was gloriously decked in fine garments, lit by bright lights and facing a gold plate which it is alleged was the centre of the manger. The Padre said a prayer. Countless people were flocking in to the Church all the time. Like the tower of Babel it was. One down to earth comment when we got outside was that "the biggest bloody rogue and vagabond after seeing that could not fail to believe that the New Testament is true and it all did happen nearly two thousand years ago". The other manger where the ass was put we found as the cellar of a house.

Left to wander round ourselves and saw workmen making figures, crucifixes and chains out of mother o' pearl. These were between 30/– and £5. A few of us climbed a church steeple to look out over the meadows and green fields where the shepherds watched and tended over their flocks. These fields are so sacred to the locals that they are not cultivated at all. It was a stirring sight.

Returned to Jerusalem. Visited the Church of the Dormition. This is supposed to be the greatest piece of ecclesiastical architecture in the world. The Virgin Mary's tomb is here.

18th May 1944: a monk played to us for half an hour on the organ and it was perfect. The old man asked me if I could play and the monk was only too pleased to oblige. The chaps said afterwards that I was nowhere near as good as the monk. Very beautiful in the new part of the city. Went up the Mount of Olives passed the most remarkable First World War cemetery for Jews. It is set in a hill side overlooking Jerusalem and is well kept. What a sight. All of it was surrounded by olive trees. On top of the Mount we had a look at the University and below lay one of the finest panoramas. The old and new Jerusalem. The Commissioner's house could be seen in the background.

On the other side of the Mount we looked over the Dead Sea and away to the mountains of the Transjordan where Moses was believed to have written the ten commandments. It was all just like a colour film.

Leaving the Mount we followed the usual pilgrimage route of the cross and went round all the stations of the cross to Calvary. No one had a camera.

Then went to Gethsemane. At the entrance is the Church of All Nations. Every country in the world contributed something. Great Britain gave a coloured window. The rock where Christ knelt to pray was railed off and behind it a huge man-sized portrait of the disciples all asleep. This picture is placed in the church so as to allow the moon to play on it at certain times. At Festival times this is done. I got a leaf from an olive tree and we all left to return again to Calvary. There is a huge church on each of the seven stations of the cross and on the very top is the Church of the Crucifixion. It was packed with people of all nations. Two at a time were allowed in to see a gold-plated coffin where Christ was said to have been laid. There was a long queue to get in and all over the church were other queues, people of all nations in all kinds of dress. Went to the Wailing Wall but were asked to keep a distance.

6th June 1944: told today that the Allied Invasion of Europe had started. We realised at once how fortunate we were to have been out of any theatre of war for nearly four whole months. Rome had fallen on the 4th June but this important event was soon in the shade with the landings. We are told the place is on the Normandy coast.

16th June 1944: urgent and surprise move ordered for whole Regt to Quassassin area again, Camp Tahag. Under canvas, very hot, loads of bugs and a few sand storms.

24th June 1944: what a mid-summer's day. Must be 100 degrees or more in the shade. Left for Amiyra, near Alexandria. Water rationed.

25/26th June 1944: two days out in Alex.

28th June 1944: embarked in the same old "HMT *Derbyshire*" otherwise and for ever known to us as the "*Altmark*" on which we left Blighty so long ago.

There was not much of a naval escort, but we had an uneventful journey to Taranto, arriving on 3 July. So ended another phase of our travels – a peaceful one, but it was not without its anxious moments.

PART FIVE: ITALY AGAIN

3 July 1944 to 28 March 1946

3rd July 1944: disembarked Taranto. The harbour seemed to us a hopeless shambles. Even so, there was an air of excitement as we saw units of the Royal Navy getting ready to leave. Destroyers were hooting and signals flashing everywhere. Assembled on the quay and set off on a long march to a place called Nassissi. This was a transit camp. The facilities fitted about half the number of troops which passed through and we had a job getting a shower and you were rationed for time for washing. Food lousy. Transit camps are awful places. Everyone mixed up with other units all the time and you are forever running to the orders board to see what is to happen.

4th July 1944: told we are here 48 hours to rest.

5th July 1944: marched to Nassissi station and entrained for a concentration area called Villa Volturno, not far from Caserta. There was little left of this place after the bombing. It looked a bit like H.G. Wells film *"Things to come"*.

6th July 1944: our worst fears are being realised. With air superiority, there is less need in the eyes of our Lord and Masters for 40mm Bofors and each Bty in the Regiment has to forfeit one troop for a refresher course on infantry work. Those not transferred to infantry would be engaged more on ground shoots and supporting infantry than against aircraft but obviously available against the latter if need be. What a mess.

8th July 1944: Bty parade. No reason given. One could have heard a pin drop. The O.C. gave us one of his better dissertations on what a marvellous performance we had put in both in Africa and Italy. We had heard all this before and most of us were concentrating more on how many times his monocle would drop before he was finished. He had us all feeling ten feet high by the time he had finished when it was obvious the reason for the parade was to break the news to those about to leave. The Bty Sgt Major read out the troops involved. Our "B" Troop was saved. There was a veiled hint that this development could well be the thin edge of the wedge which would mean the end of the Regiment 115 of which we had really become quite proud.

10th July 1944: all new gear and guns arrived with some new vehicles. The mobile Bofors were new. Semi-mobile ones must have come from some other unit. Bags of ammo.

12th July 1944: gun drills and cleaning equipment in the blazing heat.

20th July 1944: moved as a Bty to a Div. concentration area at Bavagna, staging near Rome on the same night. After travelling through very beautiful country we arrived at Gualdom known to us as the mine. We had never been in a Divisional concentration area before and felt something was brewing. Here we were with the rear echelons, Div. signals and all the other attached to a Div. H.Q. when we were supposed to be moving to a forward area.

21st July 1944: Major Gen. Shears spoke to us today and broke the news gently and with some obvious regret I thought. One Bty was to be trained for mine work and bridge building, one for traffic control duties with the Provost and the other for ground shooting and anti-aircraft. The latter was to be the mobile troop of each Bty. We clicked for Traffic Control. The General said he would do all he could to keep the 46th Div. together and wished us well in our new jobs.

15th August 1944: for a week – instruction in traffic control, using men as vehicles. It was drilled in to us that traffic control, day or night was essential to good discipline on the march and there would be times when the control points were forward in uncomfortable situations.

16th August 1944: left for duties in a forward area going through Foligno, Belmonte, Casanova, Tollerino, Serravalle and Macerata to the East Coast Sector of the 8th Army. Had some mail – first for many weeks. In all letters from home, Enid had always sounded cheerful and Mother and Father never said too much about her condition but the sad news was she died on 20th July and was buried at Dringhouses. This came from Rev. Basil Smith, not home so I do not know any details. I thought for a long time about happier times together and the long struggle under war-time conditions to look after her at home. I wonder when a letter from home will catch up with me. A letter from Phyllis to say that in her canteen work in Rhyl (she is Ministry of Defence and reserved) she has become friendly with a chap – a Cpl. of all things – who has asked her to marry him but she would not give an answer until she heard from me. I always thought it was the male who was the aggressive one but here was an ultimatum. How the hell can I make my mind up in our present mess about getting married whenever the war is over and God knows there's no sign of it ending yet. It seems a long time since I met Phyllis whilst climbing the Cader Idris from Barmouth on a CHA holiday in 1938. What a turn up. It seems I am going to be one regular letter short for the rest of the war. I must stop these notes as I feel all mixed up and must write home.

18th August 1944: first site at Fabriano and Sessa Ferrato. No sign posts – only our Div. signs so first thing to find out was where did all the roads go? It was surprising the number of drivers who shouted "Where to so-and-so mate?" Convoys seemed to know what they were doing. It was here we met a detachment of Popski's Private Army. They were a mixture of all sorts and had operated with the Long Range Desert Group. Quite mad some of them.

23rd August 1944: very hot. Ordered to San Lorenzo in Gothic Line and to find the Provost Unit. I had to attach myself and ten men for all purposes. It was here we had our first rude awakening about the much maligned "Red Caps" or Military Police. They had had awful casualties on this traffic control lark and we soon changed our mind about them. The Sgt said he would like me to go out with him that evening when a big change over in the line was to take place. I knew this was a long slow job, platoon at a time, coy by coy, Bn by Bn, and so on. Could take hours and you hope in the meantime Gerry does not start anything. We set off in his Jeep and had to stop twice for heavy shelling before San Lorenzo. The whole operation went off smoothly and we returned in the small hours. He seemed to know the terrain like the back of his hand. It was clear there had to be some order in these change-overs.

25/26th August 1944: sent to control a diversion 1.5 miles long. Had to stay until last light and ordered to keep what was little more than a single track completely clear for some tanks moving up. One end of the diversion was under observation, the other was not. I thought it odd there should be any movement of vehicles during daylight but we soon got the hang of what was required. It was a quite impossible task without some form of communication. I sent a runner back for the No. 19 set. He returned to say it had been "borrowed" for another cross-roads and so there was only one alternative and that was to find a signals unit to grab a Don 5 and a cable with all of which we are familiar. Who would have a mile and a half of cable to spare? By mid morning with near chaos on the diversion we had scrounged enough cable to join together a couple of old Don 5s. Letting the chaos continue still further, we set off and laid the cable from the drums and did so without a vehicle. When we were about half way along a Col. stopped me and asked me "What the hell are you laying cable along here for Sgt?" I explained to him that we were attached to the Provost and I had orders to keep this diversion clear later in the day and to control traffic on it meantime whereupon he told me I would be better employed doing just that and not "messing about with cable laying". I had to tell him that there were certain one way stretches of the diversion and since we could not see each other at either end, the only thing to do was to lay a cable to communicate along the one way parts. He muttered something and drove off saying that I ought to let nothing more move forward until some blockages further back were cleared.

I left two to continue cable laying and testing every so often and went to see what these obstructions were. What I saw would have been a gift for any enemy aircraft or for that matter artillery. Vehicles were trying to pass each other when clearly there was not enough space, vehicles were on their side off the track with the crew fitting up winching gear to get out and it was utter chaos.

I ran back to the cable layers and was overtaken by a Brigadier in a Jeep. He seemed to know more about us than the old Col. did. He gave instructions that nothing further had to move up the diversion until I had personally checked all was clear. He asked if I had been told about the tanks later on and I said I had. He then told me that they would not arrive until last light.

By late afternoon when we were drenched with perspiration, terribly hot and hungry. The road was clear and we had established a system of quick signals on the Don 5s unless it was necessary to speak. Things worked well with each end being in the picture on all movements and whether to let one go or stop them etc. We felt quite proud of ourselves, despite the chaos of the morning. Some food arrived and we then took turns in manning the Don 5.

By last light all was quiet. Too quiet. No sign of any tanks. Decided to stop any movement from front to rear in case the tanks appeared. By 9 p.m. the most terrific stonk started all along the diversion. The Germans obviously expected some movement along the road after dark and part of it was under observation. We lay in the nearby ditch until the shelling stopped and then set off to test the line. The first break was 400 yards away. The problem was finding the other end to join. It meant going forward to find the line and then come back. Luckily we had enough spare cable for joins if they did not exceed a yard or so at the most. There were four breaks up to half way along the diversion and we managed these, blind as it were, in 40 minutes. Only one of these mends failed to get through when we attached the wrong wires to each other. We still could not get through to the other end so had to go on when another stonk started. It was extremely accurate shooting. We had to abandon the next break – before finding it – and lay in a hollow not far from the road. It seemed an eternity before the shelling stopped and several times the earth shook near us and we were showered with soil and gravel. The screech was sickening. When all was quiet and that awful feeling comes on you wondering when the next one will come, we decided to make sure that what we had already repaired had not been undone by the stonk. We went back therefore and after about 300 yards, tested with no reply. The question then was which way to go, knowing that there were breaks in each direction and no communication at all for the tanks. We calculated that we would be about midway along the road when the second shelling started and from there back to the start point we mended another five breaks. Some of these were easy when both ends of the break were found quickly.

It was now nearly 10.30 p.m. and we were distinctly weary. Communication was in order from the start point to about half way so we set off again. When we arrived at the place of the second stonk, we tested and all was well to the start point only. Still no noise of tanks. You hear these a long way off at night time. We pressed on and found three more breaks which took us to within 400 yards of the other end of the diversion. I went on to tell Borrill to leave his set and help with finding what must surely be the last break. I had just reached the end when the area around us was like daylight. A star shell burst and dangled over us. They were like flares from aircraft. We froze and wondered whether this was to be the start of another stonk because we had had enough. The road all this time had been quiet and the Germans must have been edgy about movement along it because there was no other target really. He might have thought there were troop concentrations by the road.

When the star shell went out a few seconds peace remained before another horrible stonk. It would have been suicidal to continue looking for breaks so we lay in a gully which gave some protection but not a lot. The very earth shook around us. You don't think at a time like this whether the shells are plus or minus for the road – you don't care really – but we wondered what state the road would be in anyway and here we were trying to establish communications at each end of a road which may be impassable. The bursts of this stonk seemed to be the far side of the road. When all was quiet again we heard heavy mortar fire towards the front and small arms of both sides all of which seemed more than the usual nightly skirmish. We were in the dark about what was going on in the forward area anyway, but presumed if it was an attack, then we could understand why the road was shelled.

We set off again, feeling now despondent about the number of breaks we could find and insulating tape had to be rationed with each break. My hands were wet, not with sweat but with blood and the greater part of the skin had come off three fingers on each hand. The breaks we were still to find became more painful as the night went on.

I lost count of the breaks mended before midnight and was relieved to find only the odd shell had actually landed on the road which was of fairly soft earth and could easily be negotiated by vehicles and certainly by tanks but where were they?

I think it was about 1 a.m. when the line was through and mercifully in time to take a message that a blood wagon was on its way down. It took a long time to do the mile and a half because of the holes but there was some satisfaction in that. I almost wished there had been something to stop the wagon through but all in all we felt we had done something as ordered. At first light I had a message by D/R to stay put, that two reliefs were coming and that the road must be open for 7 a.m. when three troops of Churchill tanks would arrive. Something had gone wrong somewhere for us to be told they were expected the previous night. Nothing had to be coming down from the front at this time. I returned a message that a bulldozer was required urgently or some help from the Pioneer Corps to mend a number of the larger shell holes which luckily the ambulance earlier had circumnavigated more by chance than anything.

Morning came, crisp and fine and we were dead beat. The tanks arrived and at some speed in a cloud of dust which could probably be seen for miles sped by with a wave from the turret. Only three vehicles had been held up at the other end to enable them to go through and that was the result of our night's work.

We walked back through Sapriano and found the Provost unit. They already knew the tanks had gone through and we were highly complimented on the job. A breakfast of sorts was followed by a wash and sleep after I had found a first aid post and had my fingers bandaged.

3rd September 1944: the war is five years old today. Good news from Europe but when will it all end? Ordered to Golendino to man a crossroads until relieved by the Provost. This was like Piccadilly Circus and traffic came at us from all directions. By now we had the idea and kept it all moving but the dust was so severe that the duties had to be cut down and undertaken more frequently for shorter periods. Something to cover the nose and mouth was essential.

Did a spot of looting in Golendino. Nearly all the houses were badly knocked about but we helped ourselves to all sorts of nick knacks with no one any the wiser. I pinched an excellent piece of material which was a cover for piano keys and a few photos of the area. Found some wine and dealt with an unopened bottle between us.

5th September 1944: moved to Salleducia and Il Peggio. The larger pieces of German Artillery were still ranging on this place and whilst the stonks were nowhere near as bad as the diversion, it was an unhealthy spot generally. We had two crossroads to control here, with three on each at Il Peggio and Salleducia. Standing exposed on the large cross road was far from pleasant as one or two heavies landed near. We were relieved by the Provost and within an hour one of them was killed outright when the crossroads had a direct hit. I only knew him casually but he had been with his detachment through the desert and the outfit were clearly moved by his sudden loss. This shook us all considerably. I had been standing on the very spot an hour earlier.

10th September 1944: sent to Montefiore, not far from Marciano. Montefiore was a village on a high feature and was very difficult all of the time. Even though the front was creeping slowly forward, the peaks of the Gothic Line stand out so much that they can still have the attention of long range guns when you least expect it. Sporadic shelling only.

11th September 1944: issued with a No. 19 set with which we were all familiar. Plenty of spares. Ordered to move forward to "Oxford Circus" immediately behind the Hampshires who were to take Gemmano. This looked to me like a miniature Cassino. The T.C.P. (Traffic Control Point) was at a huge crossroads in about 6 inches of fine dust. We had not been there very long before we realized the crossroads was under observation. There was to be no running into the ditch here because the worst thing to happen would be a traffic hold-up or jam and with the blazing sun on the windscreens, it would all be a fine target. We tried to comfort ourselves by saying that one would have to land right on the crossroads. We directed two large convoys, dealt with lost personnel and set up something of an information bureau to boot before late afternoon. Whilst shelling was spasmodic it was never really heavy like the diversion and we all remained at the crossroads, one hour on and two off, with masks round our mouths and nose, the whole day.

12th September 1944: rumours that the Hampshires are to attack Gemmano. Fairly heavy traffic most of the day both ways. Whether or not the Gerry has moved some of his artillery further back we do not know but this is the first large crossroads target we have been on which has attracted so little attention bearing in mind it is in full view of several peaks in the Gothic line. Heard the Hampshires have taken the hill and lost it twice. They must be spent by now but we heard a final attempt was to be made towards last light. At about 6 o'clock something made me move away from the crossroads when there was not much going on and I lay with my binoculars behind the scrub. I had not been there long when a text book smoke screen was laid at the foot of the hill and our 25 pounders started. I could not see any movement but mortar and artillery fire went on for some time and then all was quiet.

19th September 1944: reception on the No. 19 set was becoming difficult in the hills but we managed to receive a message ordering us to Vallechio by the Marrechia. I made a mistake in map reading on this trip and was well and truly lost. I drove in to a Field Artillery position and they put us right. What signs there were at various road junctions had been either destroyed or removed and I was half a mile out. We had torrential rain at this site and the T.C.P. was a quagmire. We had no one stuck though.

21st September 1944: ordered to Serravello. No sooner there and had just completed vehicle camouflage when another message came to move to the Republican State of San Marino. This is a separate state and so far as I knew we were not at war with them or they with us but it was fully occupied just the same. When Italy capitulated we presumed this little state did the same. We ought to know more. Many of the inhabitants had fled and there was a spot of looting again here. Mainly wine. We slept on a cobbled pavement next to an R.E. lorry and found out next morning that it contained 3 tons of H.E. From this site we saw the result of some terribly wrong tactical move on the part of 1st Armoured Div. tanks. We could not count them – certainly 20 – all knocked out on the crest of a hill. This is not tank country anyway. San Marino and area is very beautiful although damaged a lot.

6th October 1944: move to La Villa. This took us right through the State. Its loveliness was marred by a few dead bodies and terrific damage. We travelled part of the way with rags tied around our faces. The bodies had decomposed and were black. The stench was unbelievable. One chap was sick in the back of the Bedford. More difficulty with the map but we eventually arrived near H.Q. and were put in an old farm near B.H.Q. Here we rested, cleaned up, had some mail at last, and the No. 19 set repaired and waited for the next call.

7th October 1944: sent for by C.O. Found the Sgt Major and Adjutant there on arrival and wondered what was afoot. The time on the diversion, the pounding we had had and the tanks were the last things on my mind but the old man came straight to the point and told me that I had been recommended for a "mention in despatches" for the episode – along with the others. I asked if it was in order to tell my parents and the old man said it would be preferable to wait until the "mention" was an award rather than a recommendation. I came out with a pat on the back from the Sgt Major which made the day. His praise is sparing and he is a veritable sod at times. This showed his other side. He has his North West Frontier medals, years of service all over the place and all this to him I suppose is just another war. He does instill into each one of us though an immense pride in the unit and all in all is worth his weight in gold really. He is the kind of chap that when he is around, you sort of feel safe whatever happens, the Sgt Major is here. Wrote Mother and Father despite what the old man said.

9th October 1944: all ranks paraded first thing to be told by C. O. we were to revert to "Bofors" for a period, the length of time he did not know. There was a big push coming and we would be wanted for a number of V.P.s (vulnerable points). Our guns and ammunition were on their way and would need no servicing etc. on arrival. Deployment orders later. There was some relief that we had been taken off traffic duties and our attachment to the Provost ended for now at any rate.

10th October 1944: ordered to Santarcangelo, to a crossroads below a de-bussing point. Found it without any difficulty. Very hectic, the area being under shell fire as we entered it. No aircraft about. Lot of artillery fire going both ways. Near misses for the crossroads. Towards last light the Germans must have guessed troops were de-bussing as half way through the D.L.I.'s de-bussing the whole area was plastered and they were mauled before even starting. Some walking wounded passed through us and ambulances came up at last light.

11th October 1944: last night was the most hectic for some time as the shelling was so incessant there was little if any sleep throughout. Our own 25 pounders are to the rear but joined the clatter all night. Our trenches are deep so we are O.K. but it is the awful whine and crunch followed by a wait for the next one which wears you down. There is only one road to Santarcangelo and everything for the front must move on it so the Germans are determined to hold up reinforcements and all the rest of the paraphernalia which moves at night.

13th October 1944: orders to move to a forward F.D.L. but to call at Bty H.Q. first. No names mentioned. Quick moves mean nothing to us now and all went smoothly until we became stuck in the mud getting the gun out. Had to winch it out and lost time. Last to arrive at H.Q. I was surprised to find it so far forward. On arrival attended "O" group and was given latest situation report and position of front lines as of today. The end of the thin blue line on the map touched a little village called Mondiano – my destination. It was the most forward one of the Bty and whether or not it was a compliment or a kick up the backside I shall never know but the C.O. said I had been chosen for this one because it was a difficult recce.

I had been hoping for a rest after Santarcangelo particularly when I heard the others had had it fairly cushy or at any rate one of the V.P.s further back. This was one of those occasions where one has to do as ordered and grumble afterwards and it was no use my saying my map reading had gone off a bit or something like that.

I left instructions and map references with my Bdr. and set off with a despatch rider. It was shortly after 2 p.m. and not a lot of daylight left in which to recce. When about 1000 yards from what looked like Mondiano from the map, we had to dive in the ditch for shelling. We were at a fair height by now and in the cool late afternoon the whole scene was eerie, looking across a fair sized valley to high ground either side so it seemed we would have to be outside the village. Then it happened. From the valley below came a terrific mortar barrage – big ones – and we could just hear the moan of them. The village was smothered in smoke from end to end. This was a depressing start as we had to get into the village to do a proper recce. We waited a little and then fifteen minutes to the end of the first barrage, down came another. The D.R. a Tom Cooke had the name for being a bit of a dare-devil and he said that I could not do recces messing about up here and we had to get down there to see what was what. I knew what this meant – one of his dare-devil rides. My mind went back to that historic night when we had to go and get a fresh gun from Tabarka after Sedjenane and I kept Tom company on his pillion just for the ride. That was a hair-raising journey.

The main worry now was to get the recce done before dark. We raced down the road-cum-track to the village as if we were being chased by the police and stopped on entering the village. This must have taken all the time between the mortar bombardments because the next round started and we lay on the pavement by the wall of a big house. There was not time to try to get inside. No civilians about. They had all taken to the hills. The mortars could not have fired more accurately as the majority seem to land in the main village street and, being cobbled, the shrapnel went for long distances. All the houses and few shops looked battered with shutters hanging off, few windows whole and some with roofs ripped off.

We crept up the village and came to a chap from the Leicesters who said his HQ was in the village. He said the village had been bombarded the whole day at fifteen minute intervals. Typical German. No variation at all and this lad said you could almost set your watch by it. He warned us not to go beyond the crossroads as it had not been swept for mines and said there was an attack going on up the valley under heavy smoke which we must have taken as low cloud from our earlier vantage point. Things were not going well and the Germans were concentrating on the crossroads now to stop any movement on the roads to Mondiano.

Another problem was that not only had I to find the nearest spot to the cross roads for the gun but also to find what was best for the 19 set reception. I saw a farm house not far away from the cross roads and leaving the D.R. I made a detour of about 400 yards to it. All was locked up and the place had not been hit. The spot meant absolutely no movement in daylight but there was excellent cover for the W/T truck and Bedford. It was "Hobson's choice" really.

The next problem was to reach the farm by road. I returned the way I had come and asked in the Leicester's Coy HQ who put me on to a track higher up, without getting to the crossroads and in any case, beyond the crossroads was believed to be mined. Sometimes the Germans were careless and when they vacated in a hurry would leave their signs "*Minen*" or "*Meinfeld*" but as a rule, they did not advertise where the mines were. Anyway, this road had not been swept by the REs and that was good enough for me, the Bedford full of ammo and ten men.

I went up to the track and found it suitable, returning to send back the D.R. with a message that a recce had been completed with some difficulty, the V.P. identified and that access could not be by daylight unless the line moved forward which was unlikely from local information. I asked for the detachment by 6 p.m. and said where I would be waiting for them.

I returned to the crossing to find two of the Leicesters, the first chap I spoke to and his relief, both standing outside a building which looked like a booster generating place, fairly stout, narrow and tall. It must stand out for miles as a crossroads aiming point. I laid my tommy gun by the wall and we had a drag. Then another barrage started and the earth seemed to vibrate underneath us. These were clearly "moaning minnies" as the large mortars were called. We dived in the doorway of the building and flung ourselves down on the pile of rubble and dirt. I was in the middle. There was no screech of bombs, just the thuds and they were in line right up the hillside. These moaning minnies fire I think thirteen at a time by remote electrical control and the shells come out of a revolving wheel which contains 13 separate muzzles. There is a battery of these, the result is devastating at 13 a time and they were very accurate.

The other two were lying by each wall. I was in the middle. Something seemed to tell me that one of the salvos would hit the building. The earth was shaking and the shells crept like an eternity to the top of the slope. They hit the side of the building, the crossroads and inevitably the top of the building where the roof had already been blown away. Down came the rest crashing on top of us. Whether another shell followed to catch the side wall when the roof was gone I don't know but there was a blinding flash, terrific bang and heavy debris came down. By now we were almost choking with thick dust. I tried to look up and could see nothing. I rubbed my eyes and found my face all wet with sweat and as I could still see nothing I made sure my eyes were actually open. I prodded them with my fingers. I think just for a few seconds I must have been blinded because gradually, although twilightish outside, a grey mist of thick dust returned. I then found I was weighted down by something in the small of my back. I could move my shoulders but not the bottom or legs and when I did manage to swivel round I saw huge concrete boulders and large stones across me. I had nothing more than a dull ache but when I tried to wriggle out, a severe pain came just above my seat and right down my left leg. The shelling continued and there was nothing to do but lie there and wait until it ended. I shouted to the other two and one answered that he was covered with debris but had not been hit. The other one said he thought he had been hit above the bottom and in the small of the neck where there was a hot stinging feeling. I could just reach him and felt for his neck. How he was not in extreme pain I don't know but there was a hole about as big as half a crown in the middle of his neck. I could not reach his emergency dressing so I had to use my own. As for his bottom, without another field dressing I could do nothing. The other chap could not reach his dressing because he could not lift himself up for the debris. The whine thump and crash of the mortars continue on the village and road. By now my bottom, small of the back and left leg felt a bit numb and I wondered what had happened to me. I thought at first the whole building had collapsed about us but managed to look up to the top and saw the whole roof missing and part of the top of the wall. It was obvious then that the shrapnel bursts had gone outwards. I considered myself lucky as had I gone in first I think I would have gone to the wall rather than the middle when the bombing started.

To say that we were frightened would be an understatement. We had had shelling before but nothing like this. My tongue and throat went awfully dry, the palms of the hands wet with sweat. It was a horrible feeling. Then it occurred to me how were we to get help if none of us could move the debris from over our backs. I reached over to the wounded one and felt for his neck. I shook him but he did not answer and much to my horror I found he must have been bleeding badly because the field dressing was soaked.

I asked the other chap if he could wriggle himself free and try and get to his HQ for some help and a stretcher. I saw him in the dim light reach forward and clasp a big boulder for an anchor and tried to pull himself forward but he was well and truly jammed. Then nothing short of a miracle happened. I heard a voice outside and could just turn my head to see in the doorway a padre in his shirt sleeves. His dog collar seemed to shine in the dark and he pulled away at the debris. I told him the one on my left was wounded and needed a stretcher. I heard him puffing and panting to move the larger boulders and at last I felt as if a ton weight had been taken off me. He told me to dash for a cave on the opposite side of the road about 100 yards towards the village. I stood up and found it very painful to put one leg in front of the other never mind dashing for the cave so I crawled across the road on my belly pushing on the elbows and feet but the going was rough and I tried to stand again when I reached the other side. Half crouching by the scrub and rocks at the side of the road I worked my way down to the cave and when about 20 yards from it there was an almighty crash and the next thing I knew was that I was deposited at the mouth of the cave having been literally thrown there by the blast. It was unbelievable that I was not hit. A medical orderly in the mouth of the cave saw me coming he said I was "raised off the ground for the last yard or so".

Inside the cave was a pathetic sight of civilians huddled together, saying their Rosaries. There was no panic. The medical orderly had attended to some of them with slight wounds. There had been no time to escape the village for these people and I gather we had rounded them up and put them in the cave for their own safety.

A lull in the shelling enabled me to get to the R.A.P. (Regt aid post) where luckily the M.O. was still in attendance and he examined me saying that I would have some heavy bruising but nothing was broken. The wounded one by then had arrived at the R.A.P. and he was in a bad way. He was the first to go back when the ambulance came but the road was in such a condition, all movement was delayed. I don't know what happened to the third chap – I never saw him again.

It was clear now that the detachment could not possibly keep to the time I had suggested so I stayed in the Leicesters H.Q. the rest of the night although I could get no sleep.

14th October 1944: my detachment arrived in the small hours. An extra No. 19 set was sent with instructions that we were to leave the Bofors and resume traffic control over a 1.5 miles single stretch of road to Mondiano. Congestion at the crossroads had to be avoided at all costs and I could confirm this with some feeling from our experiences on it the day we arrived. This was only yesterday but it seems an age. An armoured column was to approach before last light. Trouble is everything here seems to happen at last light. Wounded have to go back – after of course the blood wagons have come forward, food and ammunition have to come forward and then if in the middle of all this we have to deal with armoured vehicles, we were in for a rough time if any shelling resumed.

At 7 a.m. I was on the crossroads and Major Gen. Hawkesworth came along. I had not seen him so close before. He asked me my unit and if I had had any breakfast. I told him I had not and he told me to go back to the village, shave and have breakfast by Jove. He told his driver to move off and I called him back when the jeep halted immediately. I told him that the road ahead had not been swept for which information he thanked me and simply told the driver to "keep to the middle of the road". They disappeared round the comer and within seconds of his departure, a barrage started on the mined road ahead. It was as if the Germans knew the top brass were visiting the front. The old man had no one else with him.

Had no difficulty with the road and both sets worked well. Six Spitfires attacked the valley about mid-morning, presumably the moaning minnies. Hope so anyway. It was all over in half a minute. Marvellous sight.

15th October 1944: the O.C. spoke to me today and said it was unbelievable that I had been in the building on the crossroads and asked how I was. I told him I was very stiff, could not bend down much but was just bruised according to the doctor. He then broke some unfortunate news to me that the recommendation for a mention had been refused by Div. I wish now he had never told me because I wrote home about it. He said it was true in a sense that gongs were rationed and he was sorry it had not come off. The number of awards for the whole Brigade were too many apparently so they had to be pruned.

19th October 1944: the 2/5th Leicesters were relieved today by a unit from 4th British Div. and we had to return to the Bofors near the crossroads whilst the de-bussing and movements took place. Rumour has it that there has been a break-through on the plains near Rimini and it is gaining pace but the war on the plains has to keep pace with progress in the mountains.

21st October 1944: at 8 a.m. received a message by W/t with map reference to R.V. with the Bty and to move immediately. There was great excitement at the map reference – a place called Taveleto, well away from the shelling which was like a tonic. Spirits rose. There was an extra urgency to move this time. The journey there was beautiful and the local peasant folk kind and generous in their humble sort of way. After a clean up, we were told that each Sgt could take 15 men, a truck, rations etc. and go on a roving commission for one week. After some discussion, we chose Senigallia where the allowance of petrol would just about fit. This was a pre-war riviera on the East Coast. War damage was heavy when we got there, no amusements, cinemas etc. Bathing was not possible but all in all we had a good rest just messing about for a week.

31st October 1944: whole unit moved to Bertinoro where the news was that we were to revert to infantry. This was received with mixed feelings but many felt it was inevitable since we had had air superiority for so long and there was little if any need for Bofors 40 mm anti-aircraft weapons.

The C.R.A. came to address us and said we had played a vital role as a forward movement control mobile unit as well as Bofors earlier in the campaign and the usual clap about how we had every reason to be proud of our achievements. He emphasised the difficulties of strategic war in Italy, with part of the opposition being on flat plains and part in difficult mountain terrain. He said we would be split up in to various units according to age, rank and experience.

5th November 1944: moved to San Vittore and Fratta. Handed in all equipment except weapons.

9th November 1944: moved to Falerone in Forenzia. It was bitterly cold and the village high in the mountains. The panorama was marvellous and despite the intense cold, life was bearable and we had a large house as a billet and also were receiving high altitude rations. No fuel for fires apart from what we could scrounge by way of twigs and odd bits of trees. No village amusements or wine bar. To liven things up we put on a concert and it was so successful that the old man thought it might have to be repeated. I played or tried to play "Rustle of Spring" and "*Buona notte Mama*" a favourite Italian song of the times and everyone sang. I also had to accompany Lt Bliss on the fiddle and it was horrible. I could do nothing about the piano which was not all that bad but he did not have his fiddle properly tuned. It still brought the house down though as we both plodded on out of key with each other. Then he tuned it properly to which everyone clapped and we played "ave maria". I got a bit lost in the accompaniment but again it brought the house down. We had one or two good singers and it was not a bad concert from amateurs.

11th November 1944: we met our first "mad Figaro" today and treated ourselves to a village hair cut. He spoke a little English and for a bar of chocolate he and his mate would sing the barber's song from Figaro and his mate played a mouth organ. These two would have got by on stage and we all had a good laugh.

[*Undated*:] No notes taken for some days. Have been a few climbs and long marches and are all pretty fit.

1st December 1944: joined a large convoy back to Naples via Foligno, Terni, Rome, Cassino and Capua. Cassino was a terrible sight. The town at the base of the mountain was a pile of rubble and the REs were still engaged in the terrible task of mine clearance. The monastery looked ruined.

5th December 1944: posted to Paolisi, to 6th Bn IRTD (Infantry Reinforcement Training Depot). No one came here with me apart from some mortar specialists. Being a classified signaller, I had to go through the whole signals course again which was boring. Today we have all the time there is to settle in but I don't like the idea of starting infantry training all over again.

8th December 1944: I find I can send and receive Morse equally as well as the instructor. This is all a waste of time.

4th February 1944: posted to 4th Bn Advanced Field Training IRTD. No notes have been taken since arrival here. We have all been worked to the bone doing the whole lot of infantry training all over again which no one has enjoyed very much bearing in mind the war cannot now be long in Europe and there is still a war in the Far East. We have had a comfortable Sgts' Mess but very strict. I was sent out of the Mess one day by the RSM because I had two buttons of my jacket undone when I seated myself on his table but as far away from him as I could. He is a terror and quite mad.

A couple of weeks ago he said the standard of communications was not good enough with all NCOs and that much more had to be done to make ourselves heard above the din of battle and for that matter any kind of noise. With that end in view he had us all out on parade, spaced fairly well apart along a huge parade ground and we were to drill the person opposite also placed a fair distance away. You can imagine the confusion when we all started shouting at the same time but this was not good enough for the RSM. He produced a motor cyclist to rev up and down the line making an awful din as he had had the exhaust removed. It was virtually impossible to overcome the din if you were shouting "about turn" when the cyclist was opposite. The RSM loved it all and seemed to delight in taking it out of anyone just when the cyclist was approaching. If the chap opposite did nothing as usually was the case because he could not hear, the RSM would thump you in the belly and bawl in your ear "shout from the stomach Sgt not the throat". He was a real sod.

He must have been really hated because a week ago he was assaulted by a couple of Guards chaps stationed nearby. They tackled him in the dark outside the canteen. The two Guardsmen were put under close arrest and taken away for Court Martial. We never heard what happened to them.

We had a number of night exercises which were solely for moving without noise in difficult terrain and in typical RSM fashion – we assumed he had chosen the areas – we had to move through woods where bracken was thick and so on, making a frightful noise really. The instructors would place themselves well away in order to discover when we were first heard and then we would get a slating the following day at lectures etc.

We have come to San Martino for tactical training all over again and to do a Junior Commando course of six weeks. Fortunately, we all seem fit.

8th February 1945: told only NCOs are to go on the Commando course with the rest on a later one. Moved outside San Martino in to Nissen Huts. Kits checked.

10th February 1945: bitterly cold and some snow. Had to practise crawling under wire with no small pack on. Elbows and knees very sore as some of the ground was rough. Each one had a channel to himself and whilst it was not a race to get through it was just too bad to be last. Repeated this several times and then had to put on small packs. Few could manage without getting caught in the wire so we had to learn the best and quickest way to get free amidst all sorts of colourful remarks shouted at us by the Instructors.

14th February 1945: taken to a large firing range for the usual types of shoot. Application did very well. Snap shooting was bad and we all had to stay until it improved. The target appeared for 5 seconds only and you did not know if it would remain stationary or not. My target only had one hit out of five shots so I had to do ten more and got three.

17th February 1945: punishing route in bitter cold – slush and mud and all done in FSMO (Field Service Marching Order). Had a tot during one of the stops. Nine miles in all but worth double under normal conditions.

21st February 1945: all taken to a fairly fast flowing river where we saw wires erected to the other side and we had to crawl monkey fashion across. Mittens were allowed, not proper gloves. The wire was like a razor and we nearly all drew blood on the first crossing. We were nowhere near fast enough and we all had to cross several times until we were about whacked.

After a break and a brew of tea, we had to repeat the crossing with slung rifles. Anyone who dropped his weapon had to go back for it so with that warning everyone was anxious to get things right and go back. George was in front of me and in front of him was a burly type who was swaying the wire a bit too much and put George out of his stride. You have to start when the next one is about a third of the way across. What happened to George's rifle was a mystery but he must have taken one hand off the wire and it slipped off into the swirling waters. There was a bawl from the bank "Get that rifle that man" and down went George, disappeared from view and came up with his rifle. He swam to the bank and was allowed to double back to the billet in view of the conditions and temperature.

24th February 1945: back to the river again and did four crossings. This time the instructors threw into the water a bit of gun cotton as soon as anyone slowed up. This made a useful explosion right underneath you and was very unpleasant. I had one put underneath me on the last time across and was drenched. All doubled back to camp.

27th February 1945: taken to river bank again but this time had to cross on three trunks slung part over and part in the water. The width was about three fair sized tree trunks but they were far from even and the lower you were in the queue to cross the worse it was because of all the mud and slime which preceded you. I was about half way down so it could have been worse. It was fatal to actually look at the water. The middle trunk was a couple of feet over the river and whilst no one fell in, we all took our time – too much according to the instructors and had to cross again i.e. twice.

3rd March 1945: went to a small ravine where the sides were about the size of a normal house and ropes were suspended from the top. They hung loose down a vertical bank. We first had to scale the rope without any gear on which was bad enough. When at the top we ran along about 500 yards and had to slide down a muddy bank. This was about the same height as the ropes and not quite vertical except that at the end there was a lip which shot you out. We were told to put some speed in to their operation because there was a large coil of barbed wire at the bottom of the lip. You could not see it as you went down and could do a nasty injury. We were relieved to see two staff standing at the end of the gully to give an extra shove if they thought you were going to land on the wire. Another added incentive as it were was that through all this you had to keep your weapon dry and clean so there was no question of steadying oneself down the chute.

8th March 1945: bitterly cold. Taken to an open area not far from the river crossing points and ropes and chute spots. This was to be a trial run of doing the whole lot in one go. Added to the various sections done was to be what the Sgt Major called a "touch of realism" in that if anyone failed anything or was slow etc., he would be fired at by the staff who would be in concealed positions. We would then be labelled "dead" or "wounded" as the staff thought fit.

The target time for the course was set at 45 minutes. This meant going off in sections to avoid a queue but the thought of the river crossings by wire and trees as well as the rope climbs, the chute and then firing on a range after crawling through the small hoops of barbed wire was not an inspiring one. I was in the middle section to go and all went well until we came to the river crossing both ways by trunks. The other sections had really left the mud and several fell into the water. There was to be no running back to barracks despite the cold. They had a tot of rum though.

I had no falls except that I was caught and bawled at as "too slow Sgt. Get a bloody move on" when going over the river by wire. I thought my arms were going to drop off and the worst thing to do is just stop for a breather. They threw in a big slab of gun cotton just under me and I was drenched. Our section did the lot in 55 minutes and had four "dead" and six "wounded" leaving only five unscathed.

Our instructor said the course would be done again on our last day but one and must be in 45 minutes with considerably more life put into it. Let off for the rest of the day.

15th March 1945: had a cross country run a.m. Rough going for mile and a half each way on the flat with features in the middle. Every man for himself like the Fell races years ago. Came sixth with a few cuts and bruises. I took a short cut which I thought at the time was a clever thing to spot but fell down a ditch into a pile of rubble and sharp stones.

16th March 1945: repeated the full physical course in 49 minutes and all went well, even the shooting.

17th March 1945: sent for Orderly Room early. Posted to a Depot H-Q. Signals Infantry Reinforcement Training Depot as an Instructor. Very relieved.

18th March 1945: moved to IRTD near Udine. Not a bad spot. Rest of chaps posted to 1st Bn Kings Own Royal Regt., so lots of farewells.

29th March 1945: given seven days leave and went to Bari. Place dead and nothing much to do. Could not even get to sands and too cold for the sea.

10th April 1945: first classes arrived for training as signallers. Some knew Morse and the 38 set and these were signalled out for exercises. Comfortable mess and no shortages. Parcel caught up with me from home. Reels of cotton of all colours and some scented soap. Far too much. Party of us went down through the town out to a small village to flog some soap, cotton and two or three of us had de-loused blankets underneath great-coats. I did not feel happy about this as we would have been for it if caught but it seems everyone is on the make. Told today that the Yanks will pay £6 for a bottle of gin or whisky. Called in a wine shop and showed one blanket and the cotton. Immediately, the young girl sent for "mama" and in a matter of seconds we were in a small room at the back of the shop. I got 12/6d for each reel of cotton and a quid, that is about 1000 lire, for one bar of soap. The old girl went mad about the blankets and we each got 5000 lire. She said she would make clothes for the bambinos. Being thus relieved, went in search of food in the town but all closed down and settled for a bottle of vino and bag of nuts instead.

3rd May 1945: everyone knows from the news that the war must be in its last hours and the Italian Cease Fire was announced today. Not a great deal of celebration oddly enough as the fighting in Germany was not over yet and at the back of everyone's mind was the Far East and wondering whether we would return to U.K. when the time comes or go there.

1st June 1945: No notes taken for nearly a month. Spent in general duties, care and maintenance, tidying up etc. In the early hours of the 8th May, all hostilities ceased in Europe. It was at that time I wished we had all been together – the old lads now in the K.O.R.R. – because we all seem to be odds and ends in this depot. Celebrations in the mess and a general feeling, hard to believe at first, of relief that it was all over.

2nd June 1945: vacancies drawn from a hat for leave on the Isle of Ischia in the Bay of Naples. Came out lucky and packed. Went by road. Knew none of the rest of the party.

3rd June 1945: what a lovely island. Untouched by the war, it is divided in to four sections. RAF, Navy, Army and Women's Services. Bathing on excellent beaches. Put in a good hotel and waited on hand and foot. All ranks taken off whilst on leave on Ischia so you did not know if some elderly gent swimming next to you was a cook in a local unit or the Brigadier. Come to think of it they would not go swimming with their rank but on the beach everyone was stripe-less and pip-less as it were.

4th June 1945: made friends with a cabby and booked his pony and trap for a few days. Quite a character. Very hot and clothed in the minimum set off on a tour of the island. Mountain in the middle and about 9 miles round. The cabby said his brother had stored wine away in a cave in the mountain to hide it from the Germans and that if we liked he would take us to it and sample the wine. Outside the cave would be not far short of 80 degrees and inside the bowels of the mountain about 30 degrees less so we had a problem. The wine was excellent and we had two full bottles between the four of us. The cabby had his own which he kept supping at the front. In an hour or so we were quite jolly and ready for some food. The wine store in the mountain was amazing. The Germans never found it and there must have been thousands of bottles packed in crates lined with straw and hundreds just loose.

5th June 1945: barber called first thing at the hotel and started shaving everyone who felt so inclined out on the balcony in the early morning sun. He sang as he shaved. Went swimming and lazed about all morning. Too hot to move much in the afternoon.

6th June 1945: the idea of one beach for the females doesn't work and we find them bathing on a beach of their choice so we went round to their beach to see what we could find. Had the same cabby and called in again in the cave for some wine. Found the women's beach crowded with RAF and Navy types but few Wrens and Waafs seemed to be about. Very wise I should think. Lazed about, had a swim. This beach was so enclosed with high cliffs that it was fun to swim out a bit and make noises particularly blowing hard on the water at water level with the mouth. The echoes went on for ages. George Ounsley as usual making the biggest noise lost his teeth, top set only. This would be in about 7/8 ft of water and none of us were very good at getting to the bottom to see if we could spot George's teeth, so we stayed and marked the spot whilst George went off to get a couple of young lads having explained to them that his "*denti perduti*" – teeth lost. They swam out in a flash and dived many times without success. Poor old George.

They were army teeth so he had to report them as lost.

8th June 1945: lazed about all day in the sun. Ate a whole melon each.

9th June 1945: return to Udine via Rome Ancona Venice and Mestre and found myself posted to CRU (Corps Reinforcement Unit) No. 2 British.

16 July 1945: no notes taken for six weeks. Nothing of great importance has happened. Boring duties but comfortable mess.

17th July 1945: posted to 1st Bn Kings Own, 10th Indian Division. Rumour has it that the Indian troops will not be expected to have another Italian winter and may go back home.

21st July 1945: Orderly Sgt for day.

7th August 1945: attached to 14/16 Garwhali Rifles for Internal Security work and posted to Gorizia. Nasty situation developing between the Italians and Yugoslavs as to demarcation line and we have to keep the peace. There is the Morgan line, named after a General, to which no one seems to agree.

29th August 1945: nothing unusual the last couple of weeks. The carriers have helped a lot to avoid demonstrations of rival factions meeting. Told today we could go to Venice for seven days, a unit at a time.

30th August 1945: set off for Venice in 3 tonner. Our hotel situated on the Lido. Helicopters still spraying the canals. There are 132 and the pong from some is awful.

31st August 1945: went out with Sgt Barrington to get our bearings. In St Marks Square and the church. Very dark and overpowering inside. Coffee or something like it in a road side cafe.

1st September 1945: beautiful day. Went out in a Gondola. Started with a row about the charge as apparently the Americans pay more than we do for a ride. Compromise settlement made and we moved off. Under the Bridge of Sighs and by the Ducal Palace and St. George's Island.

4th September 1945: lazy days in and out of the sea. Terrific sun. Good hotel and service. Waited on hand and foot by Italian waiters.

15th September 1945: Land LIAP confirmed (Leave in addition to *Python*). Went by truck to Milan and entrained for Calais. The devastation in parts of France, blown bridges etc. was no worse than we had seen in Italy. The only disappointment on the journey was that we went through Switzerland in the dark and all we could see were the twinkling lights high up in the mountains. We stopped for a long time on the border and civilians threw bars of chocolate at us and wished us well. A troop train coming back from U.K. was opposite us for a time and we had a running commentary of what things were like at home, food rationing and so on. One chap had spotted someone he knew in the carriage next to us and shouted to him that his wife had left him for a Yank and he was volunteering for the Far East.

Journey well organized with food stops etc. but bit cramped at six a compartment and on wooden seats. Arrived without incident at Calais.

19/20th September 1945: arrived Folkestone. The sight of the White Cliffs was a moving one. Repeated announcements made about everyone with a weapon on him had to surrender it at the Bursar's office. Failure to do so would mean immediate return to unit. There were quite a few handed in, Lugers and other types of pistols.

On arrival at Kings Cross I sent a telegram to Mother and Father to say I would be on the 10.10 p.m. train which would be in York 2.30 a.m.

Train absolutely packed and I could not find a seat. Had to stretch out in corridor which was a line of bodies. Could not sleep for the foot traffic to the loo. Managed a seat at Grantham and promptly fell asleep.

On waking I found the time to be half past three so I set off to find a guard to see if the train was running late or if I had passed York. I rubbed the window outside the compartment to see both river and silhouette of what certainly didn't look like York Minster. Alas it was Durham Cathedral. The next thing to find out was if the train stopped at Newcastle which I thought it did. Kept awake with some effort. De-trained at Newcastle and had a tea. Several hours wait for next train south and arrived in York 11.15 a.m. Father had come down to the station to meet the train on which I was sound asleep.

17 Pulleyn Drive seems just the same but no Enid and Mother and Father look that much older. The long struggle with Enid's illness under war-time conditions had taken its toll. Had a huge lunch and fell asleep.

21st September 1945: had a leisurely walk up Dringhouses in civvies to look at Enid's grave and took some flowers. Pint at the Fox on the way back.

I wrote no more notes while I was on home leave.

25 October 1945: in the middle of a game of tennis at St Chad's, Father came over with a telegram to return to "Bolzano" with details of unit etc. Spent some time in evening going over every map we had to discover where Bolzano was and found there were three to choose from. I had to report to the RTO at Charing Cross first.

26/27th October 1945: set off back again. Father saw me off. The RTO put me in charge of twenty chaps to take to Bolzano and I asked him which one had the 46th British Div. stationed there but he did not know.

Entrained at Calais after a good crossing and again passed

through Switzerland in the dark to Milan and Verona. Here we hitched a lift to the first Bolzano and spent the night in a transit camp. No one knew where the 46th Div. was. I was given instructions how to get to the second Bolzano by train. Stood all the way. The Italians looked at us in a surly sort of way, probably because they felt we ought not to be there anyway, were travelling free and taking up room for many civilians who could not get on the train. I tried my German on a lady and asked her where Bolzano or "Bozen" was and she said there were a lot of troops at Bolzano in the Dolomites, much further north.

31st October 1945: arrived at the correct Bolzano and was duly ticked off for being two days late. I proudly produced the telegram and suggested it might have been better if the Bolzano in the North had been specified as there were others.

4th November 1945: good billet. These are the old H.Q. of one of the German Divisions. Excellent mess facilities. The German POW waiters could not do enough to oblige. Made friends with some of them on the telephone exchange.

5th November 1945: arranged some language tuition with the telephone people for an hour a night in exchange for some chocolate and cigs. They seem a harmless enough crowd and showed us photos of their families and houses etc. They were much older than we were and had only come into the army late on being taken from their post office technical duties which was further evidence they must have been scraping the barrel towards the end. One chap I was particularly pally with was a P.O. Engineer in Berlin and had lost his house and all family in the bombing.

7th November 1945: instructed that Montgomery's non-fraternisation order applied to us and as our visits to the telephone exchange had become known, they had to stop. I phoned the exchange to explain as best I could.

9th November 1945: work in hand was to clear the vineyards and some of the roads of cable. To do this, we took two truckloads of POWs with armed guard and made them go into the vineyards which had not all been swept whilst we did the roads which had been swept. Some booby traps were found in the vineyards which I marked and reported to Regt to clear. Not a bad fatigue this, out in lovely country and not too cold yet.

11th November 1945: Sgt Gee and I came by two motor cycles, small ones, and persuaded the German mechanic in MT to put them in working order for us. Went off to Merano for sight-seeing and had a good day. In a wine bar we talked to an elderly chap and his daughter who asked us to visit them for an evening. They seemed quite well off and not affected much by the war. Merano, HQ of the Red Cross had not been touched and explaining where they lived, we left the bar only just in a fit state to ride the cycles back in the dark.

14th November 1945: Sgt Gee and I set off for Merano and found the address we had been given. An old stone-built huge house in a courtyard in wonderful surroundings. We had a warm welcome and sat down to some nuts and wine. Then came the other daughter to whom Gee attached himself.

The meal was very welcome but I felt quite ill afterwards. Everything was cooked in a thick sort of oil. Did not bargain for being asked to stay the night but we were shown to spacious bedrooms. The one I had was obviously used by an American, the place being scattered with his photos and highly polished brown shoes under the bed etc. I slept about half the night, wanting to be sick but could not.

15th November 1945: strong black coffee and a roll for breakfast. Gee was all smiles and said he was coming back again as he had slept the night with the other daughter Maria. The one we met in the pub was not much cop and to satisfy his curiosity I told him I had tossed and turned half the night wanting to be sick. The mother and father insisted we stayed a while so we sat out on the verandah and he played some opera on his gramophone. All very pleasant. No problem on return to the barracks.

30th November 1945: past two weeks more cable clearing, general care and maintenance, no guard duties and not a great deal to do in the evenings.

4th December 1945: any personnel with a knowledge of German was told to report to orderly room for possible consideration for transfer to AMGOT (Allied Military Govt. Occupied Territory). About ten turned up and had names taken etc. The whole area north of Bolzano was to be covered by personal inspection of AMGOT teams, and map references taken of damaged property, graves, position of enemy gear or our own e.g. destroyed vehicles and so on. Sounded a nice job to finish with and anything to avoid the Far East seemed to be the order of the day.

6th December 1945: a truck load arrived from the Jewish Brigade, all of whom spoke fluent German, which was more prominent than Italian in the area so none of us were taken for AMGOT. Disappointed.

29th December 1945: posted to 56th Div., 24th Guards Brigade at Lazeretto, near Trieste. Modern barracks and a good billet. Many ships scuttled in Trieste Bay and harbour. Some destroyers and frigates of the Royal Navy were in. Rumours of civilian unrest due to dispute about boundary between Yugoslavia and Italy.

5th January 1946: lot of peace time bull at this depot. Can't walk across the square etc. as in the old days. Stand still for Retreat and the lowering of the Union Jack at last light. Masses of bugle calls.

7th January 1945: found a good W.O. and Sgts' mess in Trieste, open to all units and an excellent spot. Sausage and eggs, spam, table tennis, billiards, writing room, quiet reading room etc. Wrote a few letters.

9th January 1946: all ranks confined to barracks due to demonstrations in Trieste. Rumours of civilians fighting each other.

12th January 1946: went with Sgt Gee for a ride round the bay to the Yugoslav border. Wanted to take some snaps of the scuttled ships. Came to one of the demarcation lines and over the road was a huge sign "TITO" surrounded by greenery on an arch. We got off the cycles, took some snaps from the Yugoslav side – there was no border guard, building or anyone about. Then suddenly someone took a pot shot at us from the sloping ground at our rear. We were not armed and even if we had been, did not want to get involved in any incident now, so we hopped it sharp. Reported the incident to the I.O. on return.

15th January 1946: called up six years ago today. How time flies. I wonder when we will go home for good.

17th January 1946: lectures on current affairs at home.

18th January 1946: had a good tip off from signals room that all ranks were to be confined to barracks after 6 p.m. today. In other words, if going out the time to clear off was before 6 p.m. Four of us went at 5 p.m. without any difficulty to the Mess for a meal and a game of table tennis.

Just before last night we heard a commotion outside and the doors of the club were shut. Went on to balcony to see what was afoot and the place was seething with Italians. Obviously two different demonstrations had met head on. In the past there was usually an armoured car or carrier at the front of each demonstration so they were able by wireless to steer clear of each other and so avoid a fight. Something had gone wrong this time.

I have never seen civilians fighting before. It was all fisticuffs, no weapons but the screaming and shouting, pulling of hair and just one mass of humanity pushing against another mass, packed tight was just beyond belief. To say they were a rabble would be too kind. Some looked up to the balcony and shouted "*Viva Meeter Churchill*" and "*Viva Inglese*". To which there were replies of "up you too". Other colourful remarks were shouted down. In the middle of all this the carabinieri arrived and they did not spare their truncheons to try and get through. No one was giving any ground. The Italian police were hopeless and making no impression. About ten minutes later, three armoured cars from the Guards came and side by side with only inches separating them, they edged the crowd away to a junction where another three cars were waiting and they drove between the Jug faction and the Ities.

We were told to wait one hour and then go straight back to the barracks preferably in groups, not singly. This we did and on arrival back found that earlier in the morning someone had pulled down the Yugoslav flag from one of the main streets and in return, the Italian flag had been torn down from the square in the same street about half a mile away. This had sparked off a demonstration later.

23rd January 1946: asked over in groups of four to the Officers' Mess for drinks. This was quite an event and for a purpose. It was to offer certain promotion to stay on, not necessarily for the Far East but no one was kidding us about that. I was offered a place at Octu for three months in Naples after which assuming I passed I would be 2nd Lt.

They filled us with gin and some eats. There were jobs of WO 2 (Sgt Major) and commissions going like hot cakes. I thanked our hosts for their warm hospitality and said that as I had got a job to go back to in civvy street and had been away over 6 years I would rather put everything together again than stay in the army and no doubt go to the Far East. Only one took the bait and stayed on.

5th February 1946: posted on the Jug border to do guards. Had twenty men, a cook, wireless and rations for a week. Transport remained with us. Orders were to prevent smuggling of arms over the border. This meant stopping everyone.

6th February 1946: nothing unusual so far. The Jug border is round the corner just out of sight. We have two Nissen huts, wire across the road, easily moved on wooden strips. Stopped an old couple with a cart, loaded with winter hay. They refused to have the load inspected so we knocked all the hay off and found nothing. They gesticulated wildly at having to pick up all the hay but we helped them.

8th February 1946: cold. Stopped a few cars but found nothing.

9th February 1946: pile of trouble today. Last night there was some shooting nearby from the direction of the Jug post and too close for comfort. I doubled the guards, we all stood for a while, and first thing this morning one of the chaps asked if I had seen our flag. We all went to have a look and there was the Union Jack riddled with bullets. The height of the flag was well above the Nissen huts but it seemed lucky shooting in the dark. To do this someone must have come round from the Jug post by the water's edge right up to the edge of our site unobserved by the guards. There was a suggestion that we give tit for tat this evening and shoot up their post. I said we were supposed to be friendly with the Jugs and it was no use making trouble. I suppose I ought to have been a bit firmer about it and there I made a mistake. I was dozing about 11 p.m., fully dressed on my bunk, when I heard a bren firing, fairly close. We all stood to again and I doubled the guards placing guards also down by the water at the back of the Nissen huts. The Cpl. then suggested we had a roll call because he could not trace everyone and then the worst happened – two were missing. They came round by the water 20 minutes later and were nearly fired upon by the guard. They had been to attend to the Jug flag they said. I gave them a good rollicking and we remained on stand-to for another hour.

10th February 1946: despatch rider came early for me to report to the I.O. (Intelligence Officer) Brigade H.Q. the other side of the bay about 8 miles away. Here I had a ticking off because I had not reported the firing of the previous night and now there had been an official complaint from the Jugs about our episode. It was no use saying they started it first. Anyway, the old man wanted to see me and I was marched in to the Brigadier, his Adjutant and another staff Capt. I found it hard to explain why, given the wireless, I had not reported the incident when our flag was shot up and also hard to explain why I took it on myself to attack the Jug post the following night.

I explained that this was without my knowledge and against instructions. This only made things worse because I was then asked if I had put the offenders on charge and if so what was the charge. I had not of course charged them.

The Brigadier let rip somewhat and said in the present delicate situation regarding the boundary line between the two countries, nothing could have been worse, that a full report had to go to Div., that someone with my experience and so on ought to have known better. Had it not been for a good word from my own C.O. I believe I would have been charged with neglect of duty or something. Instructed to report on the hour by radio for the rest of guard.

14th February 1946: handed over guard duties and glad to clear out back to barracks in Trieste.

20th March 1946: name appeared on list for U.K. class "B" release on the 28th March Group 26.

27th March 1946: saw R.S.M. to ask permission to take photograph of retreat and lowering of the flag in view of departure tomorrow. He agreed. Got a good snap of the guard at fix bayonets with the flag being lowered as the bugle sounded.

28th March 1946: up early and packed rest of small kit. I must remember to note the route home. Trucks to Udine and train to Milan. Changed to large troop train to Villach, Seebach, Malnitz, Salzburg, Traunstein, Rosenheim, Munich, Augsburg, Ulm, Karmenstein, Karlsruhe, Strasbourg, Pagnym, Hirson, Lille, Armentières, Calais, Dover, Aldershot, Woking.

Journey well organised but could not sleep through being packed like sardines into carriages, with full kit and wooden seats again. Good channel crossing.

Parted with all kit in Woking and fitted out with civilian clothing minus a hat as I could not find one to fit. Shoes were too big but I brought them.

Every man for himself and made for Kings Cross. So it was all over. I went in as A1 and came out as A1, the medical taking about 30 seconds flat which was ridiculous really.

I could not find a seat on the train which was packed to capacity so I sat in a first class carriage. There was an army Major and an RAF type who looked at me rather sternly and said nothing. The guard came along and said I had to get out. Both officers were immersed in their papers etc. and said nothing. I told the guard I would gladly get out, as he put it, if he found me another seat. The chap I was with and whom I did not know was a bit more awkward and asked the Guard where he had been the last few years and they had an argument. The guard said he had his job to do and all that. In the end we stayed. We were not alone as the whole first class coach seemed to be packed with other ranks.

The journey was slow with many stops. It was a fine day, cool but blue sky. Neither officer spoke to us the whole way and when we got out at York I think we felt the same relief as these officers would feel – almost joy to see us go.

I had not told the family of my arrival. No taxis and with long bus queues I decided to wander slowly up the Mount carrying my cardboard box of ill-fitting clothes. The mind was something of a blank really. Here was the day one had longed for yet it all seemed so ordinary. Thornton's Antique shop was still there and the Odeon where six years before we had tried to get into the R.A.F. I felt myself thinking of how if the war had proved anything to me as an individual it was that life seems to hang on a slender thread of circumstance. My main pals who had gone to Dishforth to learn to fly before the war had not survived very long yet I tried to follow them and was turned away.

David Ashton, killed in one of the first raids on the Island of Sylt. Eric Wright shot down in a Hurricane in the Battle of Britain and Hugh Horsley, after two tours and a Sqdn Ldr, killed when landing at Church Fenton, himself badly wounded and most of his crew dead.

I stopped at Knavesmire Gates and looked up the road towards the old house in Knavesmire Crescent, then crossed the grass and walked up Pulleyn Drive.

I knocked hard on the front door with no response. I went round to the side and again no response. My fault I thought and then I saw my father in the garden digging for some spring planting. We greeted each other and he went in to wake my mother who was asleep. The tears of anxiety which had sent me on my way over six years before turned to tears of joy and I think we were all conscious at that moment that Enid was not there. How she would have loved the family to be together again.

Mother went upstairs and brought down my gold watch which was a 21st birthday present from Enid and which Mother had wound every single day of the war. It had never been allowed to stop. She said she always felt I would return to wear it. The long nursing of Enid in the war years had taken their toll. They both looked much older and Father fairly deaf now.

A fire was lit, the kettle on and shortly I fell asleep.